How Football (Nearly) Came Home

How Football (Nearly) Came Home

Adventures in Putin's World Cup

Barney Ronay

HarperCollins*Publishers*

HarperCollins*Publishers*
1 London Bridge Street
London SE1 9GF

www.harpercollins.co.uk

First published by HarperCollins*Publishers* 2018

3 5 7 9 10 8 6 4 2

© Barney Ronay 2018

Barney Ronay asserts the moral right to be identified
as the author of this work

A catalogue record of this book is available
from the British Library

ISBN 978-0-00-832407-0

Printed and bound in Great Britain by
CPI Group (UK) Ltd, Croydon

MIX
Paper from
responsible sources
FSC™ C007454

This book is produced from independently certified FSC paper
to ensure responsible forest management.

For more information visit: www.harpercollins.co.uk/green

To Kate, James, Ed and Max

Contents

Introduction

Coming Home

7 June 2018

There were times during the endless World Cup summer of 2018 when it was impossible to escape 'Three Lions', or 'Football's Coming Home', or whatever the song is actually called. Two days after England had beaten Sweden in the heat of Samara, as the World Cup wound down through to its endgame, a press release popped up in my inbox around 11.30 pm Moscow time, one of many that appeared every day during Russia 2018. This one was called 'Not Just Football' and it said that a survey by something called Vanquis Bank had discovered that 86 per cent of people believed an England World Cup win could 'unite the country'. More than half felt 'generally happier' since the World Cup had started. Ninety per cent of people felt more proud to be British. Most unintentionally sad of all, in the middle of all this unintentional sadness, more than a quarter of pensioners said they felt less lonely because of the World Cup.

Reading this on the late-night Moscow metro, eating a packet of Russian cough sweets in lieu of dinner, after three weeks away from home chasing the World Cup around this massive country what leapt out at me was: that's a lot of lonely pensioners. Also, before the World Cup came along a lot of people seemed to feel the country was disunited. And once the World Cup was done more than half of the country would go back to being significantly more unhappy.

On the plus side, at that point it was hard to see any real end to the World Cup summer. A few days later three thousand people would gather in Hyde Park to leap and bounce and hug each other and drown in the evening sunshine as Kieran Trippier put England ahead against Croatia. A combined TV audience of 62 million people watched England's last two matches. The motorways fell silent. The band of the Queen's Guards played a brass-instrument version of 'Three Lions' outside Buckingham Palace. Meanwhile *Civil Service World* magazine published an article by Sir Michael Barber comparing England's manager Gareth Southgate, who previously played as a centre-back for Aston Villa and Crystal Palace, to JFK, Tony Blair and Clement Attlee. 'Gareth Southgate showed us a different way. Unfailingly polite, thoughtful, humble, self-reflective and calm – and at the same time obviously passionate, iron-willed and determined,' Sir Michael swooned. Online data analysts recorded that on a single day in July somebody in England tried to buy a waistcoat on average every twelve minutes.

How did we get here? Or rather, how did we get to here from there? It's time to rewind two years. Let's go back, for a moment, to the worst place.

*

The thing that really stood out in Nice, June 2016, England versus Iceland, was the way the England players' faces seemed to collapse as the game wore on. Watching from close to the pitch you could see the eyes widen, the lips tremble, a look of sadness settling over the blue shirts even as they trotted through their patterns like sad, dutiful, dying horses.

It's easy to forget that England had gone 1–0 up against Iceland early on. It's easy to forget too how beautiful it was an hour and a half before kick-off, strolling down through the trees and the scrub by the roadside on one of those evenings where the air turns damp and warm and a little sickly-sweet as the light dies away.

There was a band of England fans across the middle of one of the stands, and as the players warmed up, a round of applause rippled down the seats like a breaking wave. The last patch of evening sun had faded away over the lip of the stand and as England kicked off everything seemed to have turned a lovely soft blue. With four minutes gone Wayne Rooney scored from the spot and England were off.

At which point, something else happened. Enter: the fear. It didn't take long. The weather can shift so quickly on these occasions, the texture of the air altered by a single misplaced pass. Ragnar Siggurðsson equalised after a flick from a long throw. Then Kolbeinn Sigþórsson put Iceland 2–1 up with a soft shot that trickled past Joe Hart.

Watching from the press box, we knew this game was done just before half-time when Raheem Sterling picked up the ball by the touchline. The band of England fans that had cheered the players before kick-off was up on its feet now as Sterling ran past; but this time all you saw was a row of unhappy faces, pointed fingers, bunched fists, rising to their feet as he passed.

Sterling looked spooked. All the players looked spooked, with something horribly tender in their movements, their arms and legs now a little jumbled and muddled, always somehow facing the wrong way. The fans would later say this England team 'shat it'. The pundits used words like 'frozen' and 'choked'. England teams have shat it before. But this was something more obvious, a real-time shatting. Defeat wasn't just coming. It was already there, rearranging the furniture, preparing its best lines, moving like a ghost among the players.

The next day Roy Hodgson appeared before the media in Chantilly. Hodgson was up there in front of the advert boards on no sleep, sweating and twitching and looking like the disgraced chancellor of a crisis-ridden central European state held hostage by invisible captors and forced at gunpoint to talk in a halting, frazzled voice about looking at the wider picture and being proud of this group of players.

Introduction

It did feel different. This was not just another cyclical low. This felt like the end of something, a defeat more vicious than sport usually throws up. Nobody was saying well played, better luck next time, carry on old chaps. Back in England at the fag end of the summer the feeling of alienation was tangible, not so much a call for change any more – always, always the call for change – as a kind of anger, a sense of distance from players, team, manager, an absence of any connection with these sullen, failing superstars.

Hodgson was gone. Sam Allardyce came in and lasted one game, sacked in the autumn after a sting operation by the *Sunday Times* that revealed very little of any interest beyond the fact the England manager had sat in a restaurant drinking what appeared to be a pint of wine. In a vacuum of disinterest and distaste and to a chorus of underwhelmed bemusement, the FA appointed its Under-21s' manager on a three-game trial.

*

Gareth Southgate had been at the FA for three years at the time. He was popular with journalists, but not hugely so, not the type to play the game, cultivate friends, drop stories. He was an inside man, in the chair while the FA got its head together. Those who knew Southgate best had talked about his ambition as a coach, his genuine feeling for this job. But no one had really seen it yet. Southgate wasn't the story. He was a prop, a plot device, a holding pattern.

His first act in the job was to appear before the press at Wembley and apologise for the fact he was there. A year later, just nine months before the start of Russia 2018, England's players were abused in Malta as they edged towards a low-key away win. The team bus was rounded upon. The fans staged a mass walkout before the end. Football wasn't coming home. England had a new song. 'We're shit and we know we are,' the fans sang in the away end.

And this felt like a pattern by now, a thing that was broken, but broken in such a way that we had to watch it congeal, drawing the final lessons. The point of watching England was to document the decline, to bear witness to something passing.

And so fast-forward again. Welcome to the summer of Gareth, the summer of coming home. At times it was impossible to escape that song, 'Three Lions' or 'Football's Coming Home' or whatever it's called. It was on the radio. It was there again set to an amusing internet meme. It was in the underpass at Moscow's Smolenskaya station sung by a very drunk man from the Midlands through the microphone of a busking violinist.

En route from Nizhny Novgorod airport to a very small, hot room at the misleadingly named Hotel Grand Business, I read a really excellent, detailed dissection in an American magazine of the song's influences, its chord sequence, its implications for Brexit. When I got to the hotel a group of English people were singing a song in the car park holding a large flag, baking in the hard, dry heat of a western Russian summer. The song was 'Football's Coming Home'.

The next day we travelled down for the Panama game. The stadium is set in a flat basin on the outskirts of town.

Introduction

The traffic in town was gridlocked. In the end my taxi driver turned the engine off, bought an unusually small ice-cream cone from a roadside stall and sat down on a bench to watch the people walking towards the river in search of a crossing. The people were singing 'Football's Coming Home'.

In the days that followed the coming home of football began to turn a little bizarro, a little sozzled in the heat. A blizzard of articles and think pieces and op-eds appeared examining why, how, if and to what purpose football either was or wasn't coming home, all of them bearing the same quietly teeth-grinding subtext, specifically: why am I having to write about football coming home? Someone said England's footballers represented 'the 48 per cent of remainers'. To a degree of tabloid fanfare Princess Eugenie posted a *Friends*-inspired 'Football's Coming Home' clip to her Instagram accounts, another milestone in the game's grand history. There was a flypast over Buckingham Palace to mark one hundred years of the Royal Air Force with a fleet of Lancasters, Spitfires, Hurricanes, Tornados and Typhoons flying so tightly they could spell out messages in the sky. The flypast said, 'It's Coming Home'.

And as the World Cup reached its wild high-summer peak there was a hint of something bordering on rage among Croatia's players before and after their victory at the Luzhniki Stadium, angered by England's perceived over-confidence. And also, it seemed, by the idea of 'Football Coming Home'. Deep in the sweaty concrete bowels of the Luzhniki after the match the former Spurs player Vedrun Ćorluka walked through the mixed zone past the England press pack. Players don't often stop here, preferring instead to walk through as quickly as they can, headphones safely clamped. Ćorluka stopped. 'It's not fucking coming home,' he said with a smile.

And he's right. Or not right. Or it wasn't ever supposed to be depending on your view. It seems a deeply English thing that even now there is no real consensus over the precise meaning of 'Three Lions', the drone behind the drone at every England tournament run of the last twenty-two years.

What's it supposed to be about? Winning a tournament? Hosting one? Or some warm, non-specific, indeterminate zone in between hosting, winning and being really important, whereby football 'comes home' into a fuzzy collective embrace of heartfelt something or other? The Germans seemed to get that it wasn't meant as a threat. The players in 1996 sang it on the way to the final on their team bus. You still hear it on German radio now and then, a staple of the indie-pop playlists.

Looking back now it isn't hard to see how it could have annoyed the Croatians, and indeed have annoyed the Scots and the Irish and the Welsh. Even the 'thirty years of hurt' in the lyrics make very little sense. When the song was written by Ian Broudie, Frank Skinner and David Baddiel England had reached a World Cup semi-final just two tournaments ago. What, exactly, was everyone so upset about?

That summer as England's fans descended on Moscow for the semi-final you heard the song even more: in the metro, outside a bar near Kievskaya station, walking past the rows of pavement cafés on Novy Arbat, the flashy main drag close to my flat. And it was true. Football had felt like something vital and urgent and all-consuming for the last few weeks.

I was in Russia for the whole tournament for the *Guardian*, where I've worked for the last ten years. For thirty-five days I followed England from Kaliningrad to Samara. And not just England but Spain, France, Brazil, Iceland, Morocco and many more of your favourite FIFA-affiliated nations. Football may or may not have come home in that time, depending on a strict definition of 'home' and 'coming' and 'football' and 'is'. This may or may not have been the best World Cup, best modern World Cup, the best of the Blatter-era corruption-ball cups.

Some things are certain though. It was an unforgettable thing to see up close. Russia itself was a brilliant surprise in so many ways. England, driven on by the great Gareth, were fun and admirable. And for a while, as the country baked in an absurdly iron-willed heatwave, the numbers on the 'generally happier' index must have been up there. Or at least decent, pushing the projections. Perhaps it even seems a bit silly to some looking back, all that overwrought emotion. Perhaps, and perhaps not. I don't know about you, but I'd do it all again in a second.

1

At Home with Vlad

14 June 2018

There is an agreed international formula that governs all opening ceremonies at major sporting events. The rules state there must be tumblers and gymnasts. One of the tumblers will be dressed as a giant flower. Another is a back-flipping wasp. The tumblers and gymnasts must come racing in from the corners of the stadium while a voice burbles over the PA about sport, love, families, friendship and sporting-friendly love-families.

Finally, a jarringly miscast pop star will leap onto a plinth and rap into a TV camera. The jarringly miscast pop star must be edging towards the end of his useful career, still big enough to 'own the occasion', as Gareth Southgate might say, but not quite big enough to turn it down. The pop star will be dressed in a shiny suit. His triumphant smile through his entire seven-minute performance will carry traces of panic, shared exultation on the global stage and cocaine.

At the start of Russia 2018, the World Cup of World Cups, this last role was filled by Robbie Williams – although obviously without the cocaine as Robbie is clean and clear-eyed and oddly messianic-looking these days. He was a compelling sight too on a breezy, sunny, muggy day in Moscow. Not to mention an oddly reassuring presence at the start of a tournament that had been eight years of endless intrigue in the making.

What do you pack for this? Do you need a coat? Will it snow? I'd been to four football tournaments before this one. I'd never felt afraid or anxious before. But then, none of them had ever been in a place or a time quite like this. There isn't another major nation that feels quite as opaque from the outside.

Before going to Russia I was clueless, ignorant, utterly in the dark. After going to Russia I was clueless, ignorant and very slightly less in the dark than before. Oh yes, what a journey it's been. It's strange how easy it is for a nation as vast, powerful and prominent as Russia to retain this air of mystery even now. Russia has been everywhere for the last few years, a collage of events, opinions, fears, leading statements. In my job you often spend large chunks of time abroad, catching a heavily stilted but often slightly unguarded picture of the places you pass through.

In the last few years I've been to India, Brazil, Australia, Ukraine, Poland, Switzerland, Austria, Germany, France, Iceland, Abu Dhabi, Norway, Ireland, Portugal, Dubai,

Spain, Israel, Azerbaijan and Liverpool. I've survived all of them, liked all of them. But somehow Russia was still a blank.

A week before my flight out on 12 June, two days before the tournament started, I went to the Russian visa building near the Barbican in central London. It felt exciting to be walking in through the security door, past the body frisk and the cameras. I kept expecting to be told to go away, or questioned intensively in an underground room. The woman behind the desk was jarringly helpful and friendly. No, she said, she wasn't that excited about the World Cup. She preferred ice hockey. I spent eight pound coins on a set of mugshots for the visa from the in-house booth, trying as hard as possible to look washed-out and glassy-eyed and like the corpse of a dead Soviet-era spy, a look that proved predictably easy to pull off.

For so long this had felt like a World Cup approaching very slowly with a club in its hand. Nine days before the tournament the British government was blaming Russia for the Novichok poisoning in Salisbury. Two days before the curtain-raiser, Russia versus Saudi Arabia at the Luzhniki in Moscow, I'd picked up my blank phone and blank laptop in London, both of which would be quarantined instantly on return, wiped for bugs and tech-bombs. The generic advice to those travelling included instructions on what to do if you're detained, attacked, arrested or jostled by crowds. Don't wander into darkened public spaces. Don't argue with policemen or public officials. Don't go near groups of drunk people at night. All of which pretty much ruled out my five best things to do on a fun night out.

Arriving in Russia at Sheremetyevo International in the late-evening gloom, the queues at passport control had been predictably massive, snaking in an endless loop through a huge domed annexe. The border guard had stared for ages at my passport. He narrowed his eyes. He shook his head a little sadly. Finally he gave me a small, fragile piece of paper with a stamp. I'd heard about the fragile piece of paper, the terrible consequences of losing it, the circles of bureaucratic hell. Through every sweltering airport dash of the next five weeks, the queues jumped, the aggressive body searches endured, that ragged piece of paper was neurotically cherished. I've still got it here now. Nobody ever showed the slightest interest in looking at it. I'll probably keep it for a few more years just in case.

*

The opening of any World Cup or Olympics or European football championships is always a little unsettling. I'd been going to these things for a decade before Russia. They all tend to start the same. Homesick, travel-sick, shovelled up from the end of the longest FIFA accreditation queue, you tend to cling to the familiar comforts in those first few days. Up in the gods at the Luzhniki for Matchday 1 I had the holy trinity of personal effects safely locked down: laptop, phone and FIFA pass.

Plus I had snacks. This point can't be emphasised enough. Access to appropriate snacks is a vital part of any tournament. With coffee, chocolate and crisps on your side no deadline is too tight, no two-day travel binge too daunting. This is no laughing matter. Eight hours in a controlled FIFA space where the only available food is a production line of leathery pizza at the end of a forty-minute, single-cashier queue is an alarming prospect. Early investigation had revealed the presence of the large, stoic Russian vending machines that would be rolled out across all media centres over the following week, like a new generation of Soviet tank surging across the steppes.

Beyond this all tournaments basically look the same from inside the machine. The world goes on outside, but the stadia, the buses, the media centres create their own sealed space. At the Luzhniki there were the usual endless rows of white desks, the broadcast tents, the same comfortingly non-negotiable rules on process and timings. Where are we exactly? Salzburg 2008? Donetsk 2012? Salvador 2014?

In total there were five thousand licensed media in Russia. Here they come now, an infantry brigade of sweating Peruvian TV anchors, Ghanaian radio-production teams and rumpled, handsome Frenchmen. You get to know these faces down the years. Scandinavians are almost always friendly. Avoid at all costs sitting anywhere near the endless milling hordes of Brazil's Globo TV, the most aggressively territorial species of people the human race has yet produced.

Best of all are the old familiars. There is a distinguished-looking white-haired Indian journalist I've met now at three tournaments on three continents a decade apart. We seem to always be in the same queue waiting for a late-issue ticket. Each time he just nods at me curtly, like it's entirely normal to keep bumping into one another here, as though this is the post office or the newsagents down the road.

It should be said right here at the start that sport hacks love going to tournaments. They are the pegs around which your life arranges itself down the years. This is where it all stops being a grind or a job and suddenly sport seems to fill the sky, its sounds and smells and sights imprinted in a way that never really fades. For the next five weeks this caravan of sweating humanity would travel alongside the tournament, would wander late at night across distant state capitals looking for an Airbnb without a bedroom door, would Skype home unsatisfactorily, despair at railway stations, reach the end of the line in Saransk or Samara or Rostov, and generally cling energetically to the edge of the show.

In between, many of the things we expected to happen will happen. The reigning champions will collapse, as they tend to these days. Brazil will dissolve into tears and theatricals. Spain will pass themselves to death. Lionel Messi and Cristiano Ronaldo will fail to assert their relentless celebrity domination of club football. Luka Modrić, the best midfielder in the world, will play like the best midfielder in the world. And then of course there was England, who would be re-geared by a favourable draw and an expert feat of management into something else, an object of whooping, weeping, beer-flinging adulation as the country cooked back home in the hottest summer since 1976.

At Home with Vlad

From that first day this felt like a World Cup on a larger scale. In the hours before the big kick-off Red Square and its surrounds had been seething with flags and colours. The familiar hordes of yellow-shirted Colombians and Brazilians were joined by fresh infantry divisions of Peruvians, Egyptians, South Koreans, Senegalese. World Cups are often best in those opening few days when everyone gathers in the same spot, a tangle of limbs and flags.

Stepping out at the Luzhniki metro stop there was a humid kind of hysteria in the air. Replica Messis mixed with replica Salahs. Mexicans in canary-yellow sombreros edged through a knot of costume sheikhs. Teenaged Russian volunteers shouted slogans from their lifeguard chairs ('We are very happy to see you! Enjoy the World Cup very much!'). In Moscow, this familiar coming together had a dreamy quality, bound up in the sheer scale of the place, a city built for supermen and superwomen.

Things are big in Russia. Everyone knows that. Crucially, things are also really far away. You might see the spire of a building you need to get to. You can start walking, but you'll basically never get there, your legs suddenly helpless, lost in all that planetary-scale space. Try to cross the road and after ten minutes of veering between the cars it dawns on you that the columns of tiny micro-ants in your eyeline are actually people living unknowable lives on the far pavement.

Or so it felt on that first day. The Luzhniki is Russia's footballing mothership, a huge concrete bowl laid out on the banks of the Moskva River. Here the city spreads out a little, the towers die back and the stadium lurks at the centre of a network of landscaped lawns.

And so we sat and watched Robbie. Out in the middle of all that green space he strutted in his shiny red suit. He gyrated his hips. At one point his face appeared in giant close-up on the big screen with that familiar curled lip, resembling in his moment of triumph a very handsome chipmunk-warlord exhorting his chipmunk subjects ahead of the final push for global domination, but only just starting to realise in that same moment that he's actually just a chipmunk.

A Russian soprano called Aida Garifullina joined Robbie for a duet on the dreaded 'Angels' and made strange things happen to the hairs on your neck. And everyone who was anyone was there. Including, it turned out, the one person who really mattered.

The outline of Vladimir Putin has loomed across greater, more urgent things than a World Cup over the last few years. But Putin had still coloured and shaded every part of this tournament, going right back to the start of the bidding process. Reeling this tournament in was a brilliant achievement, from the deployment of assorted oligarchs to carry out the soft politics to secure the voting, to the vast programme of stadium upgrades and city-wide facelifts.

It is hard to believe now that back in December 2010, right up to the final moments, England's own World Cup bid was considered the favourite to win the vote at FIFA Towers. A spiffy presentation had seen David Beckham,

Prince William and David Cameron offer the final hard sell to the dozing FIFA executive, pushing a blueprint that would have brought World Cup football to Bristol and Milton Keynes. Boris Johnson lurked around the fringes, as ever the harbinger of some imminent clunking disaster. And Boris it was who would appear mooching and cursing among the English press just after the vote and leak the true extent of the rout. The English bid had gathered just two votes out of a possible twenty-two, one of these the FA's own man, the other the Cameroonian Issa Hayatou, who appears not to have got the memo.

I was there in Zurich watching this unfurl, a little bewildered by the scale of the machinations. One thing was clear. This was a humiliation on the grand scale for the English, who had proved astonishingly tin-eared, hopelessly gauche in the game of influence and favour. At the time the big story had seemed to be FIFA, Sepp Blatter and the surrounding murk. This would change in an instant around 5 pm on voting day just as copy was being filed, intros nailed, stories put to bed. At which point Vlad arrived, turning the day upside down.

Putin had stayed away from Zurich during the unveiling, announcing primly that he 'didn't want to influence the voting process'. This remains arguably the best World Cup-related joke anyone would make through the entire eight-year process. The reason it was such a good joke is that it feels particularly Russian. Gallows sarcasm delivered with the driest of straight faces is a national staple:

How Football (Nearly) Came Home

A woman walks into a food store.
'Do you have any meat?'
'No, we don't.'
'What about milk?'
'We only deal in meat. The store where they have
no milk is across the street.'

Still not involved in the vote, still the owner of the not-influencing-the-World-Cup store, Putin was ferried into Zurich by helicopter convoy a couple of hours after victory had been secured. What followed was a strange, gripping piece of theatre as the leader of the world's second-largest nuclear power was grilled by the English football press in FIFA's huge central hall.

Down at the front the correspondents put their questions to the leader of the world's largest land mass in agreeably abrasive fashion. There is a tired old cliché that the English sporting press are all jowly, fag-stinking middle-aged men. Like most prejudices this one is baseless. Some are jowly, fag-stinking women. Quite a few are jowly, fag-stinking young men. There is even a generation of jowly, fag-stinking youngsters breaking through.

It was fascinating to see Putin in action. This really is the titchiest of world leaders, a bald, grey, middle-aged man in a suit with a million-man standing army at his disposal and a sense of holy imperial destiny. But Putin is an astonishingly potent presence, with a way of dominating any room simply by sitting there, allowing his silence to fill the space. 'Mr Putin, is it true that in the lead-up to this decision ...'

'Mr Putin, is Russia ready to host a . . .' Alone on his stage, Putin yawned, smiled, looked bored.

He aced it of course. Presentation has been key to Putin's success. It was a televised war in Chechnya that transformed him early on from chief bureaucrat to all-round beef-caked action man, addressing the generals, drinking toasts with the troops at the front. Since then Putin has appeared in all manner of theatrical dress-up, from judo *sensei*, to topless fisherman and topless horse rider, to riding a Harley-Davidson tricycle with the hard-Christian biker group the Night Wolves.

In 2013 he was voted the sexiest man in the world by the Russian populace. In World Cup year the electro-pop single 'A Man Like Putin' re-entered the charts, a girl-band ditty written fifteen years ago, set to poppy Euro house music, and adopted now as a thrillingly straight-faced campaign-rally song at Putin events. Sample lyrics include:

I want a man like Putin
A man like Putin, full of strength
A man like Putin, who won't be a drunk
A man like Putin, who wouldn't hurt me
A man like Putin, who won't run away.

True to form Putin didn't run away in Zurich. He also didn't seem to be drunk. And now here he was in Russia too, appearing as Robbie finished his set and drawing a collective swoon, a crackle of event glamour around the stands. Projected onto the big screen from his VIP snug,

How Football (Nearly) Came Home

The Sexiest Man Alive delivered a terse, sombre speech about the joys of football. At the end FIFA's president Gianni Infantino spoke incoherently for a few moments about the wonderful feast of joy he was personally dishing up to the world here in the shape of a glorious new ... anyway, thank you, Gianni.

Infantino had been an oleaginous and energetic president in the last three years. But he has nothing of Sepp Blatter's extraordinary will to power, his appallingly cinematic lust for glory. During the game Infantino would be caught by the TV cameras hunkered between Putin and Crown Prince Mohammed bin Salman looking like an overly attentive sommelier. At times Infantino himself looks surprised by all this. Me? Here? Sitting between two of the five most powerful people on the planet? Earlier in the day Putin had spoken at the FIFA Congress and praised Infantino for the excellent job he was doing 'as our front man'.

On the pitch little was expected of Russia's footballers at their own World Cup. 'You would find it hard to find a way through the labyrinth of the Russian soul,' the Russian coach Stanislav Cherchesov had announced as he took questions from the international press about his nation's engagement with World Cup fever.

Cherchesov was right though. This was an un-engaging Russian team drawn from a sluggish and insular domestic top tier. Russian sport was in a strange place after the doping scandal that had cast a shadow over the Olympic programme. The footballers were ranked no. 70 in the world, arguably the weakest-ever World Cup hosts. Dark talk had circled of a group-stage exit, a troubling prospect for those concerned that Russia might not engage with this World Cup at all.

And so, at long last, after the prelude and the build-up, it was time for some actual football.

*

The opener against the Saudis had been billed as 'El Gasico', a reference to the fact these two nations carry between them a quarter of the world's crude oil reserves. In the wider world they are the most tangled of energy brokers, sponsors of opposing sides in the Syrian war, but cosily aligned too, brothers in arms of the gas pipeline, the tanker fleet, the energy price index.

Oddly enough it was worth the wait. Russia hadn't won in seven games. Saudi Arabia were managed by Juan Antonio Pizzi, who had taken Chile to victory in the Copa América playing an exhilarating style of hyper-physical football. Chile's players had pressed relentlessly, bumped and bruised and harried their opponents and run like demons for ninety minutes.

In Moscow the Saudis were something else. They mooched and ambled and occasionally stood near the Russian midfielders. Russia were just too powerful, too keyed up by the stage and the moment. Yuri Gazinsky headed the opening goal of the tournament in the twelfth minute. Denis Cheryshev made it 2–0 just before half-time, standing for a while with the ball at his feet in the Saudi area before leaning inside and smashing it into the top corner.

How Football (Nearly) Came Home

The second half was a deceleration, marked out by three more wonderful goals. In the stands there were 'Ross-iy-ya' chants, a series of listless Mexican waves and a weird sense of floating above the day. Cheryshev got the best of the goals, a wonderful 'trivela'-style finish from twenty yards with the outside of his foot. By the end the score was 5–0 to Russia. In the walkways and byways around the stands people whooped and yelled. A passing journalist was bear-hugged. Outside the metro station the drums pounded, trumpets blared and two very drunk young men tried to high-five the rows of armed police and were death-stared into submission. Back on Novy Arbat cars full of glamorous young Muscovites crawled along the street and blared their horns, leaning out of windows with flags and scarves.

And so we were off. Eight years and $19 billion in the making, Russia 2018 was go. The first four days would bring eleven matches, a criss-cross from Ekaterinburg to Sochi to Samara. And then, finally, it would be England's turn in Volgograd on Monday afternoon. But it all felt surprisingly good so far. A little wild, like a trip that might just take you somewhere unexpected.

2

Waiting for Gareth

16 June 2018

And so on to England. Although not quite yet. That pleasure would have to wait until the start of the following week and the opening Group G game against Tunisia in Volgograd. Until then England's players and staff would remain in Repino, their billet for the next ten days, or five weeks, or however long it took for another World Cup to play itself out.

Nobody really knew anything about Repino. That was probably the point. It's a quiet spot, twenty miles from St Petersburg, surrounded by pine trees and streams and clouds of sleepy seaside mosquitoes, but ideal for the new realism, the hair-shirt humility of Southgate's England.

Repino wasn't even part of Russia at the start of the Second World War. It was instead the eastern tip of Finland, and still known by its Finnish name 'Kuokkala'. The town found itself swept up by the Red Army as part of the Nazi-clearing surge across Europe from the Western Steppe to Berlin in 1944. When the war ended the Soviet Union just held on to it. Goodbye Kuokkala. Hello Repino, jewel of the North-western District.

England's base there was the forRestMix Club, a scattering of panelled, low-rise blocks ranged behind a high fence. Compared with the five-star show-palaces of tournaments past the forRestMix had something studious about it, the air of a pleasantly wooded Soviet university campus, or a holding pen for elite political dissidents.

It felt about right though. The prelude to Russia 2018 had been pointedly mild, consciously low key by England standards. There were games of darts and fraternal japes with the press pack. Harry Kane filled in some gaps by speaking of his love of *Fortnite*. The wives and girlfriends hovered at the fringes, still an object of fascination for some parts of the media, but present in diluted form this time, protected by a mild tactical ceasefire.

Covering England has never been the easiest task, bound up as it is in repeatedly breaking bad news to people who appear torn always between fatalism and an irrational sense of winning destiny. The written press has often been blamed for England's failures, singled out as the reason our footballers lose to more technically adept, tactically aware foreign opposition, something that always seemed like a note of basic confusion. But there has been a sharpness there at times, a mutual hostility, with a constant demand from news desks for dirt and detail, for stories around the story.

Waiting for Gareth

This time things were different. Something strange had happened after Iceland, a process that had been accelerated through the last few years. The fact is, everyone needed a good World Cup this time. It felt like a truce had been called. International football only really exists as long as people want it to exist. The dominance of club football, the cult of personality around football's celebrity stars, the basic mediocrity of successive tournament teams – all of this eats away. Football can survive pretty much anything, but not indifference.

And increasingly England seemed to have become something else, an object at one remove. I wondered at times if this was just me. Everyone has their World Cup, the ones that seem to belong to them, where nothing quite so vast and absurdly vital has ever happened. For me it started with 1986 and Mexico and a World Cup seen through the heat haze of satellite TV, those lovely bleached-out greens and blues bounced around the world from Monterrey and Mexico City. I went to bed in tears after the disappointing 0–0 draw with Morocco at the Estadio Tecnológico, tortured in particular by the sight of Glenn Hoddle, my favourite player, curling a horribly languid shot over the bar in the fraught moments towards the end. I can still see it now, the casual shrug as he jogged back, mane flapping, the sense of infuriating insouciance. No, we don't forget, Glenn.

I wasn't allowed to stay up and watch Gary Lineker's brilliant dead-eye hat-trick against Poland. Instead I learnt about it on Ceefax at 5.30 am on Thursday morning, staring at the square green font with a sense of pure giddy joy. Defeat to Argentina was pretty mind-bending after that, although I already loved Diego Maradona because even as a kid you could see a light around him, the presence of something a little otherworldly.

By the time 1990 came around I was at Peak England. After the last-sixteen win against Cameroon I cycled down the A2 across Blackheath with a Union Jack cape streaming out behind me (the Saint George's Cross wasn't a thing yet), waving to the cars and vans as people beeped their horns. England failed to make it to USA 94 but the World Cup still belonged to me four years later. England were still mine, Michael Owen my personal project. I can still see every split-frame step of the goal in Saint-Étienne against Argentina, from the perfect little heel-flick into his path, to the way his feet were suddenly beating the turf like a flyweight battering the speed bag, the perfection of the finish, and the way even the celebration sprint is a thing of beauty, all easy balance and whirring, fast-twitch limbs.

By 2002 I was still there, but somehow a World Cup had become a kind of picnic or public get-together where you watched England beat Denmark 3–0 but also talked about Tony Blair or extending the lease on your flat. Something had happened to the players, too, or to what I thought of the players, or to how the players presented themselves. This was the start of the high Premier League years, a time when something did seem to get a little lost along the way. Suddenly the players were distant, visitors from some sullen, sealed space.

Waiting for Gareth

The feeling of a real detachment probably started around the last World Cup. In Manaus on the edge of the Amazon the travelling England fans filled the city centre late into the wee hours. But the team lost to Italy, then lost again in São Paulo to Uruguay. The goalless final group game against Costa Rica in Belo Horizonte is the only occasion I've fallen asleep at my laptop while trying to write a report on a football match. The players slipped off home and nobody really minded that much, no heads rolled. A point of vital tension seemed to have passed.

The Euros came and went. The games at Wembley that followed were strange, empty, tinny affairs. England played Switzerland in a qualifier and I watched the stands empty out even as the cheers died away after Wayne Rooney's record-breaking England goal, people wandering off to the tube, checking their phones, thinking about work and school and other stuff they cared about more. What's worse than years of hurt? Years of nothing much.

*

This time, and entirely unspoken, it felt as though a kind of stalemate was in play between players and newspapers, and indeed the wider public, a rebranding of expectation. As the World Cup kicked into gear the FA even released a thrillingly downbeat set of personal messages from the players for which they were furiously applauded. Maybe we'd all reached a tipping point.

There's nothing wrong with this England squad, we sighed in the weeks before the tournament – except for all the things that are wrong with them. And it's hard to remember a group of players so profoundly written off, so clearly un-golden, so free of the burden of hype.

Southgate's 23-man squad was announced without the faintest hint of triumphalism, glad-handing or even any particular interest. As late as the final friendly in Leeds against Costa Rica, nobody really knew who was going to play in goal. Jordan Pickford seemed to be edging it, but there were doubts after a slightly frantic season with Everton. This might still come as something of a surprise to those raised on Shilts and Clem, but English goalkeepers are a bit of a running joke in some other countries. Germans will laugh about England fielding 'a butterfingers'. Memorably, one Portuguese newspaper described David Seaman at Euro 2000 as 'a piece of meat with eyes'.

Right through the team there were question marks. Who would play as the three centre-halves? Southgate was leaning towards Harry Maguire of Leicester City, a powerful and likeable ball-playing defender with no real pedigree at this level. Maguire had famously turned up at an early England training session with his possessions packed in a bin bag. Which is fun and endearing. But at the end of it you're still turning up to training with your possessions inside a bin bag, and your opposite numbers are still Sergio Ramos, Mats Hummels and Raphaël Varane.

It was easy to look down the spine of the team and see pitfalls, holes, black-eyes in waiting. Jordan Henderson had been present for the most bruising defeats of the last few years. Re-geared by Jürgen Klopp at Liverpool into a disciplined, effective defensive midfielder, he would be England's midfield pivot, a leader and senior player now, with the stamina of a horse and, some might say, the passing range of one too.

Up front Harry Kane went to the World Cup as England's captain, best player and single greatest hope. He also went to the World Cup rusty after injury and yet to score at a tournament. Euro 2016 had been a horrible experience. Kane looked cooked, baked, bombed, gone. He had four shots at goal. He took the corners.

As for Raheem Sterling, well, nobody else felt Iceland quite like Sterling. That night in Nice was visceral. Sterling hadn't scored a goal for England since June 2015. But through it all he kept coming. And he seemed one of the happier players in an unusually settled group. 'We're just like family, really. We spend a lot of time together and we all get on very well,' Kane said at one point, describing something that doesn't actually sound that much like a family at all. But you got his point. Something was happening here.

England would play on the Monday. For now, settling in to Moscow took a little time. Our flat had a kind of crow's-nest feel to it, lodged right up in the eaves of a skinny, mud-coloured stone block on the north bank of the Moskva. Eleven floors, then up another flight of stairs, past a weird humid smell of ancient Soviet-era decay, through four separate door-lock codes and you were in. After we'd sweltered through the first muggy night, Sergey, our host, explained that the air conditioning was an advanced 'complete circulation system' that needed time to whirr up through its high-tech motors. By the end we'd waited five weeks. That must be one seriously advanced air-con system.

Instead you had a choice of either keeping the window shut and dissolving on your hot-plate nylon mattress, or opening the windows, locating a grudging river breeze, but waking up at 5 am as the traffic police hit that first vital early-morning shift of sounding their sirens while speeding up and down the embankment. Back in Zurich all those years ago, Russia's bid anthem was a pounding techno song called 'Russia Never Sleeps', a claim that turns out to true for anyone living anywhere near the six-lane Moscow embankment.

Otherwise the first few days were fraught, bordering on chaotic. When a tournament starts you feel like you're running on the spot trying to keep up with it, glimpsing the cities in passing, trying to remember to eat, trying to work out the metro, always flying to get to the stadium, the press hall, the media opportunity. And still we kept thinking about England, about Kyle Walker playing right centre-back, about the knee injury sustained by Youssef Msakni, the Saharan Messi.

Before then the World Cup would begin to clunk up through the gears. On Friday I was at the Spartak Stadium for the Argentina versus Iceland pre-match stuff. Heimir Hallgrímsson, Iceland's part-time-dentist manager, promised his team wouldn't make plans for Lionel Messi. Nobody really believed him. But it's something you have to say. I took the Line 9 metro back into town with the man from the *Wall Street Journal*, the train bouncing and howling its way down to Kievskaya.

Sustained for the last two days on media-centre Twix bars and sauce-drenched salmon sandwiches, we stumbled into the lone Moscow branch of PizzaExpress, where we ordered a range of convincing but somehow slightly wrong PizzaExpress favourites. Meanwhile at the Fisht Stadium in Sochi Spain and Portugal played out what would end up as the best game of the tournament, or at least its most decorative and thrillingly skilled.

Three days earlier the president of the Royal Spanish Football Federation, Luis Rubiales, had taken a call in his hotel. Within the next five minutes, Rubiales was told, Real Madrid would be announcing the capture and appointment of Spain's manager Julen Lopetegui. Rubiales was stunned. Then he was angry. Then he was very, very angry. He'd left FIFA's congress and headed for the airport, taking the first available flight two thousand miles to Krasnodar, site of Spain's training camp. Lopetegui was sacked before he walked. This was an honour sacking. Spain had been knifed in the guts by their own royal club.

In Sochi, Portugal took the lead through Cristiano Ronaldo. Spain played some beautiful football, all dizzying algebra and perfect little angles, to go 3–2 up with half an hour left.

Ronaldo's free-kick right at the death to square the game and complete his hat-trick was one of those moments where the world seems to stop and then slingshot forward, where you get a little flash in that pause of exactly what's about to happen. As the ball whiffled the corner of the net Ronaldo ran to the corner and made the world watch him. There it was, that arms-splayed action-god leap and howl into the camera, locking in the moment, another notch in his personal iconography.

Behind it all there was still a lurking angst about England. Marcus Rashford was fit, we heard from Repino, the last real injury doubt left in the squad. Dele Alli and Harry Kane were pictured larking in training. The players seemed calm and earnest and easy in each other's space. Still nobody expected anything, or dared to expect anything.

The next day we got to see Messi at the Spartak as Iceland came to Moscow to play an Argentina team already turning in on itself. Before kick-off on another drowsy, muggy afternoon we craned our necks and caught a glimpse of Diego Maradona holding court on a glass balcony. Maradona was present as a VIP guest of FIFA and apparently being paid £10,000 per game to sit in the bleachers looking wild and wired. This was his first public appearance of a summer that would become increasingly disturbing and would end with Maradona being discreetly edited out of sight by the TV directors on FIFA's orders. But for now the response to his imperial visage, sneering magisterially down at his acolytes, was agreeably warm. Then again, Argentina's fans are one of the great joys of tournament football. In Brazil four years ago they'd crossed the border in huge numbers, hairy, beefy, beer-sodden men on a high-summer beano. When Ángel Di María scored Argentina's last-minute winner against Switzerland in São Paulo, the Argentinians around us hurled themselves about with such fury they came roll-ing down the seats and bounced into the press box, sprawl-ing apologetically across the desks. A group of extremely merry men to our right stood on their seats and waved their penises at the Swiss fans in the nearest end like beer-sodden barbarians.

In Moscow they packed out the Spartak, a sea of lovely soft blue and white, singing their own words about coming here and winning the cup to the tune of the Russian folk song 'Katyusha'. Things started well. Sergio Agüero pro-duced a turn and a top-corner spank to open the scoring. With Maradona looking unhinged and yelling over his bal-ustrade, Iceland equalised. Messi missed a penalty. By the end the World Cup had another narrative strand, another point of tension, a star cliffhanger in the offing.

In Repino, meanwhile, they were saying Danny Rose might lose out to Ashley Young on the left. They said that Southgate already knew his team, that he wanted the play-ers to 'focus on the things they can control', which might sound like meaningless management-speak, but it's good meaningless management-speak, in a sport where quite often any idea is a good idea, any shared philosophy a good shared philosophy just as long as, above all, it's shared.

Back on Novy Arbat the World Cup continued to pass in fast-forward, with the feeling always of being stretched thin. Stuart James and I discovered the row of fun, garish restaurants along the main strip just up the hill from our flat. You often only get to eat late at night at times like this, but luckily Moscow never stops or sleeps or seems to shut its doors. We ate steak in Steak It Easy, where the waiting staff were patient and didn't mind when we tried to say things like 'Medium-rare' and 'Where are the vegetables?' through Google Translate on our clunky Russia-issue phones. Walking back down through the fragrant little strip of urban park full of meat and Georgian wine, past the sleeping drunks and the hip young Muscovites, you started to get a feel of how fun and full this World Cup was going to be. Or at least, how full of meat and Georgian wine.

Germany were also in Moscow. The next day they imploded against a brilliantly well-drilled Mexico team at the Luzhniki. It was wild stuff as Germany were overrun by a series of lightning counter-attacks, planned to the last detail over the preceding six months by their engaging and talkative manager Juan Carlos Osorio. Javier Hernández and Carlos Vela tore through the world champions. Jogi Löw stood and looked puzzled in his groovy tight black outfit and ice-white trainers. Löw came into his press conference looking genuinely disorientated. But Germany had played an arrogant first game, cavalier and undermanned in central midfield, still romping forward on the flanks at every turn, expecting to pass the opposition to death once again. By the end they had been run into the ground by a fearless, well-prepared opponent. It was a first hint of something else, of the way international football still subverts the dynamic of celebrity over the collective, how it can still at moments like this feel like pure sport.

And so we thought about England a bit more. The next day Southgate's callow, unfancied team would finally take to the field down in the deep south-western armpit of Russia. Tunisia were just the kind of opponent England should expect to beat at a World Cup, and also just the kind of slick, technical, quick-passing opponent that has given them so much trouble down the years, on those occasions when suddenly the ball is square, England start to sweat and panic, passing it between them like a burden to be discharged, some terrible, guilty secret.

Southgate liked to talk about development and creating a stable environment, but the best part of him to date had been his understated ruthlessness. The lancing of Wayne Rooney, jettisoned without a second thought, was his most exhilarating moment in charge so far. Volgograd was an excellent moment to be similarly vicious. Anything less than victory would open the scars, tenderise those old wounds, work away at the cracks. The World Cup was bullocking along at an alarming speed by now. But some things don't change. England were, as ever, an object of uncertainty, angst, and – against all better judgement – hope too.

3

Victory on the Volga

18 June 2018

The opening week of Russia 2018 had been breathless. Already the World Cup had a certain tone and texture. Russia felt huge and grandly arranged. Travelling around it was like being a small part in a vast, orderly machine. The football itself was even better, with some fine goals and gripping finishes, and a certain freewheeling vim. The first few tentative articles had begun to appear asking whether, yes, this was already the best, the greatest World Cup opening seven days since the last great opening World Cup seven days.

At which point, enter England. Ah yes. We've been expecting you. 'They're ready,' was Gareth Southgate's verdict as his players stepped off their spiffy-looking team jet in tracksuits and hoodies the day before the match. He was right too. We were all ready by now. The Tunisia game had been nagging away at the back of things, lurking beneath the colour and the constant motion.

Most obviously, England just needed to win a game. Their tournament record in recent years was, frankly, terrible. Seven matches and six years had gone by since a team containing Scott Parker and Joleon Lescott had edged past Ukraine in Donetsk in front of a home crowd that had chanted 'Ross-iy-ya' at the start and risen to applaud Roman Abramovich in his box.

Under Southgate there had been a cautious sense of improvement, albeit in a slightly deathly, mannered way. From October to January England had gone 450 minutes without conceding a goal, including successive 0–0 draws against Brazil and Germany. It was steady. It was suffocating and controlled and nicely presented. But was it actually any good?

It's easy to forget now, but back in Volgograd the mood was tense, angsty, fearful of another early exit, of leaving this World Cup without making a mark. The trip from Moscow took an hour and a half on a clunky, cheerful Aeroflot. I left on the day of the game, after Germany versus Mexico the night before, cabbed out to Domodedovo before breakfast by a taciturn middle-aged man with his radio dial set to Moscow's disco hits of the seventies. As we crawled across the river he began to drum along on his steering wheel with an unflinching intensity to Gloria Gaynor's 'I Will Survive'.

The flight was packed with familiar faces. A BBC production crew filled out a bank of central seats. The man from the *Daily Telegraph* sat in front of me and made witty, urbane conversation while I pretended not to be terrified of taking off in planes.

In departures there had been England flags and caps and replica shirts in the queues for water and crab-flavoured crisps, the usual travelling pageantry. Two years ago in Lille I'd noticed something different about England fans at the Euros. A younger crop had emerged, teenagers in replica tops and old-school trainers, drenched in a cloud of marijuana smoke on the trams, up for a lost weekend in some medieval market town.

They weren't in Russia though, or not yet anyway. The English people edging through arrivals were the more staid type, the middle-aged regulars who get their tickets through the FA scheme and who follow the tours and chatter in a clubbable way at the hotel buffet.

Downtown Volgograd wraps itself around the river, split at various points by its wide, marshy banks. It was much hotter than Moscow here, the kind of heat where the air feels so thick you can almost hear it open up and slurp shut behind you as you walk around town. As we pulled into the forecourt of the homely, dog-eared Hotel Yuzhniy my taxi driver leaned across and gave me his card. 'Anything happens to you here,' he whispered. 'Anything. You call me.' At the time it seemed a fair enough offer, but then Volgograd is a slightly strange kind of place. Or at least, it's as strange as you might expect. It's probably up there, around about par for places that were almost entirely razed to the ground during the most horrendous city siege of the industrial age.

Volgograd was Stalingrad in its previous life, the

bloodiest European battleground of the Second World War. By the end of the siege of Stalingrad 800,000 people had died and the entire Wehrmacht 6th Army had either perished or been abandoned by their Führer to cold, hunger, disease and imprisonment.

There are of course tales of heroism too. I was always struck by the story of the 14-year-old girl-guide troop asked to operate an anti-aircraft unit on the edge of the city. The girl guides had no training. They loaded and shot at the skies randomly. Suddenly they spotted a column of Panzer tanks just up the road, the advance guard of the approaching German army. The girls improvised on the spot, lowering their guns from the sky in ways they're really not meant to be lowered, pointing them at the tanks and opening fire. The shells flew in strange directions, but gradually some began to hit the target. Battle raged fiercely. Each time the Panzers thought they'd knocked out the anti-aircraft guns, one would spring up and fire back. Two days later when the Germans finally overran the position, they were stunned to find they'd spent two days fighting children. The girls are now enshrined as Russian heroes, stalwarts of the Great Patriotic War.

Volgograd has been rebuilt in piecemeal fashion. You can still feel the shadows. It's a dusty, low-rise place dominated at one end by the vast, terrifying figure of *The Motherland Calls*, an 85-metre-high prestressed-concrete statue of a giant woman with a sword, dedicated to the Stalingrad dead. The main thing you noticed this time, though, was the flies.

How Football (Nearly) Came Home

The flies were prodigious, a product of high-summer conditions on the marshes. Checking in at the Yuzhniy I met my first small swarm, swallowed my first mouthful, picked the first few out of my ears. Heading into town I had to break into a run when the swarm density got too heavy to bear. I ate a shrivelled, angry-looking hamburger in a Soviet-era hacienda-style restaurant where an unidentified chemical was spritzed from the ceiling to keep the flies off. On the way back I bought a phial of concentrated menthol oil from someone advertising herself as a 'gypsy' and poured it over my head.

At least it was something to focus on. It can be nerve-racking going to report on games like these. This is why you're here, the kind of occasion that marks out your years doing this job, moments you will always remember. You want to enjoy it, to get it right. Or you want to do the opposite of completely cocking it up. One or the other anyway.

*

The Volgograd Arena was on the other side of town at the foot of the Mamayev Kurgan, the high ground above the city. Waiting for the bus I found myself next to Glenn Hoddle, who was polite and friendly while I made fawning, hero-worship small talk and tried to keep my thoughts away from that appallingly limp shot over the bar against Morocco in 1986. Glenn was also having problems with the flies, which had been attracted in great numbers to his hair. I offered him some menthol oil. He said he had a towel he was going to wrap around his head while he was on commentary.

The England team had dropped two hours before the 9 pm kick-off. It was the team everyone expected, but still it was exciting to see it there on paper. Pickford in goal. Back three of Walker, Stones and Maguire. Wing-backs Trippier and Young. Henderson as the midfield pivot. Alli and Lingard in unusual half-in, half-out attacking-midfield roles nobody really knew how to describe: backtracking run-shields, attack-curious space-fillers, galloping halfway sprint-men. In front of them Raheem Sterling would play as a No. 10. Harry Kane was England's centre-forward, the one obvious sharp edge at the front of all this careful landscaping.

The press box at the Volgograd is lodged high up in the middle tier behind the dugouts. It's a weird feeling watching the players come out on nights like these, people you last saw at Old Trafford or Goodison or the King Power doing shuttle runs and turning to wave at the fans behind the goal. As ever the England end had assembled the familiar bivouac of painted flags. It's impossible not to twist your neck and follow it around the ground, a tour of the nation through Southampton to Hartlepool, Swindon to Bury.

Tunisia had beaten Libya and Guinea and squeaked past Congo to get here. They were in Russia without their best player, Youssef Msakni, and with an attack led by the bulky Wahbi Khazri, once of Sunderland, lately of Sunderland Reserves. This game was everything for Tunisia too. Belgium were the heavyweights of Group G. Panama were the filler. One of these two would make it to the knockouts.

Volgograd was the World Cup for both of them, front-loaded right at the start.

It was dark by now, the air warm and heavy and sweet. The crowd had thickened. The players were out again looking prim in their white jackets. As the anthems rumbled around there was a moment to stand and watch the flags and take a breath. And then, with the usual rush we were off.

At which point something strange happened. England started to play, the front four a whirl of movement. Henderson was on the ball straight away, shuttling forward with that upright gait, like a cavalry officer galloping through the ranks. With three minutes gone he floated a beautiful pass into the path of Raheem Sterling veering in behind. The ball bounced across to Lingard right in front of goal. His shot was blocked by Mouez Hassen with half the stadium already on its feet.

At which point something else unexpected happened. An enormous grasshopper-style insect clumped down on the desk in front of Danny Taylor, just to my right, sparking a state of controlled uproar, eased only when the grasshopper-style thing was carefully swept off the desk and onto the back of someone's head down below.

England kept swarming forward, playing in that contained little spell like a team beamed down from the clouds. Another ball over the top set Lingard free. From his cutback Sterling, who was offside, produced the most astonishing miss, skewing the ball wide of an open goal. For a second the evening seemed to sag. Sterling grinned a horrible, pained grin as he ran back and you wanted desperately to run on and give him a hug and a pat, albeit that would have probably led to some form of arrest and incarceration.

England kept pressing. And with Tunisia looking utterly muddled they found another weak spot. Young punted in a hard, flat corner from the left. John Stones headed it back powerfully. Hassen clawed the ball straight to Kane in front of goal, who spanked it crisply into the back of the net and raced off towards the corner flag.

The red shirts romped and bounced and piggybacked. In an otherwise poker-faced press box there was the odd quiet slap of the table. Hassen walked off in tears, his shoulder pinged. And so it carried on. Lingard somehow missed a chance to make it 2–0, scooping wide right in front of goal in genuinely shocking fashion. I almost choked on a peanut. Down in front of me one of the nation's leading sports writers briefly held his head in his hands and said something best represented as a series of asterisks.

But everything was great, perfect, brill, decent, fine, right up until ten minutes before half-time when England fell apart at the back and Tunisia equalised. It was a moment from nothing. Fakhreddine Ben Youssef nipped in behind Kyle Walker. Walker swept his arm backwards and caught Ben Youssef on the side of the neck, a moment from the full-backs' playbook, the casual half-foul down by the corner flag for a nothing free-kick to stop the game. Not there though, not as a centre-half in a World Cup where referees had been instructed to look out for the sneaky grapple, the pinch and the tug.

Ferjani Sassi took the penalty, kicking his heels up like a

dancer before gliding in and rolling the ball into the corner. And so England began to fret a little. For the first time the players took a breath. Kane was wrestled to the floor in the area and leapt up waving his arms, the familiar frieze of the panicked, sweating England footballer, forever wronged on some foreign field.

Half-time felt a little wild up in the bleachers. People kept saying things like, well, they had it, they had that, it was there. England had played really well for half an hour. Then they'd looked down. The cracks had begun to show, the machinery to creak. This was a young team. But more than that it was a team that had been slightly jerry-built, a team of odd-jobs and might-yet-bes.

Walker, Kane, Alli, Sterling and Henderson were the stars, blue-chip regulars at Champions League clubs. Otherwise Pickford was a punt on talent. At thirty-two Ashley Young probably shouldn't have still been playing for England. But here he was still playing for England, and playing well too. Others were Premier League part-timers. At least five of the starting outfield players had come up through the levels in some way, spending time in the lower leagues, taking a step back to go forward. Even Dele Alli, who eight months earlier had played like a golden god against Real Madrid at Wembley, still had those ragged edges from a youth spent with MK Dons. This had looked like a weakness before the tournament. It would feel like something else by the end.

The second half began at one-tenth speed. It chafed. It grated. For a while it felt like being dragged very slowly through a strange kind of mud. There was the odd groan. A middle-aged Brazilian journalist began to Skype someone in the row in front of me. England kept the ball, but they didn't look like they wanted it, this thing scuttling at their heels, asking tricky questions, passed between the players like a difficult guest at a wedding. The minutes ticked down sullenly. I ate the second finger of my Twix-style product and stared at the screen in front of me, wondering what I was supposed to write on it. How to call a night like this with half an hour to go?

Steadily the game broke down into its endnotes, possibilities dwindling, last things checked off. With twenty minutes to go Sterling left the pitch having run himself to a stop. With ten minutes to go Ruben Loftus-Cheek came on, a fine young England player but also a strange one, surely the first to be pressing for a first-choice creative role at a World Cup with just three league goals and three league assists to date.

England had been losing traction. But there was another little rev of the engine as Loftus-Cheek began to run at the left side of the Tunisia defence, bumping defenders away, taking up those clever little half-spaces. For the first time Gareth came walking out from the dugout to the edge of his chalk rectangle down below us.

It was a little odd to see him out there on his own in his shiny-backed blue waistcoat. I'd been there at Southgate's his first press conference as England manager. We'd come to Wembley to yawn and feel underwhelmed. At that stage he was pretty much a sub-plot in his own appointment, which was really the saga of Big Sam's very sad, jowly, cross, funny defenestration. Gareth the blazer, the place-man, was meant to be the punchline here.

But something else happened. Southgate apologised for his predecessor, a fairly brutal move if you think about it. He looked stern and pensive, like the kind of junior-school deputy headmaster who stands up on stage to make a speech when the school rabbit has died. But he spoke calmly and with a kind of intimacy about the sport he still loved but sometimes didn't like. He didn't grandstand or overplay his hand. We left thinking, OK, well, Gareth. That was different.

In the months that followed there was something courtly and enjoyably old-fashioned about Gareth. Later in the tournament he would compare England's injury situation to 'a scene out of *M*A*S*H*'. Not *ER* or *Casualty* or something from the current century. His most enduring nickname is 'Nord', after Denis Norden, a TV presenter nobody under the age of thirty-five has ever heard of, because his voice was deemed 'posh' by his team-mates at Crystal Palace, just like – naturally – Denis Norden. Try explaining that to Phil Foden and Jadon Sancho, Nord old chum.

But Southgate has an edge too. Several times he told us, almost as an aside, that he had nothing to lose in the England job, that he'd reached a stage where he didn't fear what might happen next. He didn't shout or bang the desk or scowl magisterially. But he was ruthless in the best pos-sible way, freed from the constipated thinking, the sense of hierarchy, of repeating the same old failing patterns. He dumped Wayne Rooney like a saggy old IKEA sofa in an A-road lay-by. He refused to pick ailing celebrity players like Jack Wilshere and Joe Hart. His squads were increasingly made up of biddable, willing, uncomplicated young men. Southgate had consulted assorted elite sport gurus, including Owen Eastwood, one of the architects of the 'No Dickheads' policy in New Zealand rugby. England had become increasingly a likeable, personable group of players. A key point being, they didn't have any dickheads.

It was remarkable that Southgate made so little of his own destiny in all this. In Volgograd England's fans sang 'Three Lions' before kick-off, and during the first half and the second half, and ten minutes after the end as it jangled out over the PA echoing around the half-empty tiers and stands. But Southgate actually lived 'Three Lions', lived the coming home, missed the penalty kick that capped off the high point of the coming home. Watch the video to '3 Lions '98', the World Cup follow-up, and the opening minute or so of the video is basically about Gareth. The song is about Gareth. That penalty, the awkward, upright run, the scuffed shot, the crumple as Andreas Köpke saved. This was the most notable public incident of the first half of Southgate's life, the moment he became a minor note in the popular culture, the thing that football and sport and the internet and music and England fans would remember him for in memoriam. Southgate never really mentions it much, never complained, never seemed that bothered. But Russia 2018 was, whether he said so or not, the chance for a personal exorcism.

How Football (Nearly) Came Home

Not that you'd know it. For once English football ducked the chance for a painfully over-wrought soap-opera narrative. Instead Southgate focused on the team and on the details around the team. Which was a good thing, because he made plenty of mistakes in Russia too.

He made mistakes against Tunisia, who had shifted their own midfield at half-time, getting close to Henderson and stretching England's supply line thin. It was a smart, disruptive move. England's formation asked Henderson to play more or less on his own, providing a complete midfield janitorial service, fighting with the rhythms and tides of the game.

England didn't respond. Southgate had no obvious tactical answer to this, didn't really manage to free that central midfield again. Instead they did something else, something more Gareth. They kept calm. They carried on. They became less, not more frantic as the last knockings played out.

Previous England teams have done the opposite. It is the pattern of these things, the great congealment, an inability to resist the call of destiny once things start to sour. England did look robotic, frazzled, awkward. In the press box there were sighs and shrugs and the sound of copy being drilled out with a gathering certainty. The sky was closing in. We were done here, all set for another story that feels a bit like all the other stories.

Except, apparently not. People would call it luck, but it wasn't luck at all. Not stopping isn't luck. Not panicking isn't luck. England had planned this. They'd also planned to score set-piece goals. Southgate's data trawling had revealed something interesting. Teams that went deep into these tournaments tended to score from dead balls. This was one of the few areas a national team coach had time to train and rehearse and perfect. So England had a plan for these moments. The first part of which was to wait patiently for them.

A minute into stoppage time they won a corner on the right-hand side. Trippier punted it in hard and flat. Maguire broke away from the England huddle, the players lined up like a slightly touchy office conga line. His header was a powerful glance towards the back post.

The ball seemed to hang, to stop, to float upwards like a soap bubble. Would it ever actually come down? Did it have to? Could we just leave it there, close our eyes and enjoy the sense of time stretching out? Because something had become clear by now. The angles and charts, the maths pointed one way. That ball was going to drop out of the sky – take your time, no rush – and fall onto Harry Kane's head.

Kane flexed his neck. The net bulged. Everything seemed to blur. And suddenly we were done, players collapsing, referee walking off. England had won their opening Group G game 2–1, had beaten the kind of team that had given them a horrible time in the past. They'd won at the death, had won a game they might in the past have found a way to lose.

'We stuck to our shape and H has done it again,' Maguire told the TV cameras, pretty much capturing the story of the game, while also revealing that even under the greatest emotional stress, even when they themselves are also called Harry, the England players still call Harry Kane 'H'.

As the ground began to empty, that frantic post-match haze taking over, the players trooped back on and waved to the fans behind the goal. Gareth appeared a little bashfully and waved once or twice before striding back to face the media. A little numbed by it all, we trooped down from the empty stands, found the right staircase, hunted out the press room for re-writes and cadged cigarettes and the sludgy espresso from the machine. It was only Tunisia. It was only one game. But something was up here. The shape of the summer had altered just a little, England's path recalibrated. The question now was how much and how far.

4

Messi Business

21 June 2018

The day after I arrived in Russia I went along to an Argentina–Uruguay event at the South American football headquarters in Dorogomilovo in central Moscow, with the vague thought I might get to bump into Lionel Messi.

It's not that weird an idea. Argentina and Uruguay were promoting their joint bid for the 2030 World Cup. It felt like the kind of do where you might catch a glimpse of Messi being ushered in through a side door or helicoptered discreetly onto the roof. Argentina were due to play in Moscow that week. The Lionel Messi industrial–sporting complex was in town. And when Messi's in town he's an event, an occasion, a thing that has to happen somewhere.

The idea behind a joint bid was to wrap it up in FIFA's own centenary. Uruguay had been the spark that lit the fire, the World Cup's first ever hosts and first ever winners. The

2030 tournament would be one hundred years on from that first World Cup, the hosting gig sealed on that occasion by the Uruguayan FA offering to pay travel and hotel costs for anyone prepared to make the trip.

Right up to kick-off in July 1930 nobody had any idea whether the world had an appetite for football on this scale. Three weeks later 93,000 people watched Uruguay and Argentina play the final in Montevideo, where a flotilla of small boats had been ferrying fans across the River Plate for three days. After Uruguay won the match their embassy in Buenos Aires was stoned by an angry mob. And yes, the World Cup pretty much looked like a goer from there.

At CONMEBOL HQ in Moscow assorted wonks and flunkies and men in shiny power suits scuttled about the gardens. A row of beautiful women stood in a line by the entrance, ushering the right kind of guest the right side through the velvet rope. At the less desirable end of things I stood with the sports news journalists, the people who most regularly seem to know what's actually going on at these tournaments. At the last World Cup in Brazil I'd asked Owen Gibson, the *Guardian's* long-standing sports news reporter, how many people in the world actually understood the daily ins and outs of FIFA politics, the precise significance of the Cameroon delegate speaking to the AFC vice-president and exactly who stands to benefit from such an alliance. My own estimate was around nine in total. Owen has since moved on to get a proper job at the main paper. Which leaves about eight of them.

We watched from the wrong side of the rope as the

delegates and VIPs chatted and patted each other on the back and ate food from elegant trays. Messi wasn't there, of course, but Javier Zanetti was, looking magnificently well groomed, a racehorse-level human with an absurd glow about him, like a man made entirely from vitamins, soft calfskin leather and essence of handsome.

I'd come in the vague hope of some Messi colour, but also just to gawp at the basic idea of a semi-distant Argentine World Cup, a delicious but also oddly haunting prospect. Diego Maradona would be seventy years old when it happened. Messi would be forty-three, a cosseted ambassadorial figure waving bashfully from the stands, beard a little grey, paunch swelling above the hem of his shiny blue suit.

The idea of Messi being that old still sounds absurd, just as the idea of him doing anything other than play football is frankly alarming. Only one thing seems certain. When Messi does finally die, aged 146, he will simply vanish like Obi-Wan Kenobi under a goatskin shawl in some Nepalese mountain retreat, surrounded by acolytes dressed in robes, chanting quietly about assist totals and completed dribble stats. Whereas Cristiano Ronaldo, on the other hand, won't die at all, but will instead endlessly regenerate, the last element of life on earth to evaporate in a cologne-scented puff as the sun finally melts the sky and all organic life is consumed. Except you won't see it because you'll already be dead.

Too much? The thing is Russia 2018 did feel like a staging point for the greatest player of the modern age. And yes, I do mean Messi. It's a description I'm not going to bother to justify. First because there's no need; the visual evidence plus a working brain is all that's required. Ronaldo is good in a way I understand, which is equally majestic, which may even be grander at times, more effective, more successful, more adaptable. But it does essentially boil down to being very, very, very good at football in quite a humanly comprehensible way. Whereas Messi comes from somewhere else entirely. In philosophy there's a concept called subjectivism, which states that the only person who can really know what it is to be a certain person is that person himself. Thomas Nagel wrote a famous paper called 'What is it like to be a bat?' In it Nagel says it's impossible for humans to come close to feeling what it must be to be a bat because every part of the bat's brain and nerves is wired differently, its experience entirely unknowable. Well, that's how I feel about Messi. He's a bat. As an average human I literally cannot imagine how it feels to see the pass, to move in that way, to be able to play with such ease.

Together Ronaldo and Messi have been a blessing, a shared sporting era. At times this star two-hander has seemed a little overwhelming, a pair of elite athletes sucked into the machine, restyled, made over, presented back to the world as some vision of ultimacy, an icon to be fawned over.

Of the two it is only Messi for whom the World Cup is portrayed repeatedly as an unscabbed wound, a point of failure. Ronaldo gets a pass on tournaments now. Portugal won the Euros. They're not expected to win World Cups.

Four years previously I'd watched Messi wander off the

pitch at the Maracanã after Germany's victory in the final, shoulders slumped, mooching his way past a giant screen announcing him as the player of the tournament. This felt like a commercial-committee decision, a fawning after celebrity, one for Budweiser, McDonald's and Continental. But then Messi will always be treated as an individual entity, something distant from the team, both inside and outside it.

In reality he looked shattered by the knockouts, an oddly haunted figure, always just a little apart. And yet the margins are tiny here. Had Gonzalo Higuaín put away either of his very presentable chances against Germany Argentina would have won the World Cup and Messi would have been enshrined in the records as the greatest player of all time. As ever in sport meaning is reverse-engineered out of success.

If there is an inanity to this obsession with individual glory, then there is no doubt Messi felt it too. 'The World Cup is like a revolver to his head,' Argentina's manager Jorge Sampaoli had said even before the tournament had begun, a strange remark given Messi's status and indeed the poverty of the team around him.

Sampaoli had become a cult figure through his time in charge of Chile, revered for his team's vibrant, high-pressure style. With Argentina he looked baffled, lacking the energy with this ageing group to re-create that fearless press, and painfully in thrall to Messi's status. The Iceland game had kept on coming back to me through the week.

At the Spartak Stadium Argentina's fans had provided

the usual beautifully melodious spectacle, blocking out the stands with blue and white. It had felt like their day at the start. From our low angle we'd had the perfect view from behind Messi as he produced one of those astonishing lateral jinks, feet whirring across the turf, all rodent super-hero energy. Sergio Agüero opened the scoring. Willy Caballero's fumble handed Iceland an equaliser. At which point something weird happened, the game turning sallow and overcooked. Iceland waited. Argentina struggled, then grew becalmed, like a trawler beached in the ice flow. Javier Mascherano made a total of 144 passes without ever seeming to be at any stage in charge of where he wanted the ball to go. Finally Messi gave us an extraordinary moment of frailty, producing a horrible scuffed penalty kick in the sixty-third minute that would have decided the game.

Iceland's goalkeeper Hannes Halldórsson made a fine save. Halldórsson was best known previously for directing the video to Iceland's Eurovision entry. He will now be defined by something else, his own piece of sporting lore. But Messi had stood at the end of his run looking so impossibly sombre and bowed and blank that somehow you just knew he was going to miss. An hour of moping and walking and looking like an unusually sad ginger-bearded royal mouse had reached its natural endpoint.

Messi-dependence has been a feature of successive Messi teams to the extent it has now become a cliché. But this was something else, just as the air of tearful piety around Messi, the debate over how to get the most out of him, how to harness his genius, had become a navel-gazing obsession.

International football is the perfect systems-sport, an expression of the collective will. Cursed with a slow decline, blessed with the late-career gifts of a single ageing genius, Argentina had tried to make it something else. And every time Messi failed to save them the obsession would become more self-defeating.

The past is a problem for Argentina. For the last decade the national team has fed off the remains of the last really top-quality crop of players brought through during the golden years when José Pékerman ran the national youth coaching programme. The drying up of that talent is tangible. Argentina has always had a street-football culture, a dynamic where footballers are produced out of urban poverty, where cunning and trickery and skill are valued above all.

The former player turned highbrow pundit Jorge Valdano has suggested that Argentina's problems are analogous to what happened to England in the twentieth century. The street footballers disappeared. No system, no organised scheme was put in place to fill the gap. Successive economic crises have come and gone. And now the present has become a problem. Messi, the genius with the frown and the heavy shoulders, is charged with solving it, a one-man magic bullet, Spiderman in shorts. Argentina's next group game was against Croatia in Nizhny Novgorod on Thursday. It already felt like a big fat wet emotional staging post in the early days of this tournament.

*

Before then it was time to put England to bed. The retreat from Volgograd flew by in the usual post-match haze. Legs numb from three hours crouched behind a desk, I followed the rest of the media throng down through the concrete stairwells towards the divvying up of press conferences and player quotes. For the colour writer these moments are all about the re-write, the revised version of whatever injury-time-winner nonsense you've just sent to the desk.

First-edition pieces are filed at 9.30 on week nights and sent before the end of the game to meet the evening print deadline. This is the edition of the papers that goes to the places it takes longest to deliver. The rest of Britain and the internet get the rewrite. It's a bit unfair in some ways. As a wise man once pointed out, the population of Cornwall must look at their morning papers and think every sports writer in the country is a complete idiot. Here he goes again. Hasn't even put the score in. It's as though they don't even watch the second half.

As things stood my report, filed through a haze of tears and aching fingertips, went a bit like this:

Oh yes Harry Kane scored the winner and I saw it happen. That head-scoring goal. People cheered and it was good. Gareth Southgate waved at the crowd and he looked pleased and I liked him. Harry of Spurs, 25, scored the goal after 91 minutes and that's really fine, nobody's complaining. England were as a result good and not bad, just to clear that up [note to subs: please amend all refs to 'turgid same-old England' to 'sublime display of total Gareth-ball' and description of Kane as 'peripheral be-quiffed No 9' to 'lethal match-turning scalpel'].

In Volgograd the re-write was filed an hour later from the floor of the mixed zone waiting for those oddly empty moments to pass before the players turn up. It's from the mixed zone that the post-match reaction is gathered, a hastily assembled production line hidden somewhere down in the catacombs of the stadium, like the final scum swishing around the World Cup waste pipe.

After the Tunisia game we got a wave from Gareth, who does actually quite like the press. And finally Ruben Loftus-Cheek stopped for a bit and talked with a disarmingly easy eloquence about making his competitive debut. Like most footballers he is surprisingly lithe and slight close up. He's also clearly a nice bloke, characteristically so in this England group. Southgate had picked this squad in part on its receptiveness, its youth and its intelligence. Loftus-Cheek may or may not go on to succeed at Chelsea and play at other World Cups. But just talking for ten minutes you saw that he was entirely engaged in this one, already having something close to the time of his life.

After which it was finally time to leave and crawl back through the wee hours to the Hotel Yuzhniy, past the lines of off-duty trams. At least the flies seemed to have knocked off too. Back at the Yuzhniy I bought a small packet of paprika Pringles, so stale they had almost liquefied. I had four hours before the flight back to Moscow.

How Football (Nearly) Came Home

The plane was tiny, a row of single seats either side of the aisle. Nobody made you sit down or fasten your belt and the stewards chatted absent-mindedly through take-off and landing. Back at Domodedovo I got the magnificently over-the-top double-decker train for the short hop back into town. The flat was empty, with everyone else now scattered around the Russian landmass cataloguing the group stages.

Happily, I'd discovered the bottle shop at the bottom of our tower also sold bits of chopped sausage and nuts and dried figs, which took care of dinner and lunch for a while. The buying of food had been quite difficult so far. On our first night in Moscow, Stuart James and I had spent fifteen minutes trying and failing to get into the sunken, bunker-like shopping centre opposite our flat. Five weeks later we still hadn't found a way inside. It remained an enigma wrapped up inside a series of reinforced one-way security doors.

And so the games kept coming. In St Petersburg Russia kept up the fury of their opening day, swarming all over Egypt en route to a 3–1 win. Mo Salah came back for Egypt after the shoulder injury inflicted by Sergio Ramos in Kiev in the Champions League Final, an event that already felt like it happened about three years ago in a much smaller world.

As a result Russia qualified for the knockout stage and on Novy Arbat the horns beeped through the night. Men in singlets waved flags from the back of pick-up trucks. For the next three days Russia's footballers were the top story. RT (formerly Russia Today), the state-run TV network, was introduced on the hour every hour with a restless, wide-eyed wonder by the super-charged blonde robot woman of the future propped up behind the news desk.

Elsewhere Colombia lost 2–1 to Japan in Saransk, not helped by Carlos Sánchez receiving the first red card of Russia 2018 five days into the tournament. A day later I watched from the Luzhniki press box as Portugal beat Morocco 1–0 in a forgettable game, enlivened only by Cristiano's Ronaldo's goal after four minutes.

Spain beat Iran 1–0 but looked stodgy and preoccupied, as did France in another 1–0 against Peru. Kylian Mbappé scored the only goal but the real story was Didier Deschamps' cold-blooded approach. France had the most powerful squad in Russia, blessed with an almost overwhelming harvest of young talent. Deschamps had already overseen defeat two years before in the final of the European Championships. So far in Russia he'd packed his team with strength and mobility and hustle. France were defensibly powerful and technically solid. The astonishingly gifted Mbappé had played as a strictly defined impact runner off the right wing. Up front Olivier Giroud foraged and ran and held the ball, a cross between a footballer and a rugby union back-row forward. Some saw a weakness in this, a fear of cutting loose and finding the higher registers. Deschamps knew how to win at these tournaments. Time and talent would tell.

*

And still Messi and Argentina lurked behind it all. Writing articles about Messi, having some opinion on what he should or shouldn't do is always a difficult business. There are two problems here. First, this is a person who often seems to be operating under his own universe-boss-level set of physical rules. He will make a bonfire of all your predictions, reservations, words of advice, attempts to confine him to a role or a set of failings.

Plus, of course, there's them. The hordes. The converts, the zealots, those for whom Messi, or alternatively Ronaldo, represents a kind of abstract ideal, to be venerated, pored over and defended vehemently in debate. There are some subjects you learn to steer clear of on social media, muster points for shouting men (it's usually men) who blurt out their aggressively fixed positions at the slightest provocation. Messi–Ronaldo is the acme of this, a mind-bogglingly fecund source of rage and hate and mob-love. Who is the greatest? Who embodies above all the right way, the path of truth and beauty?

There are really just two interesting things about Messi. First, his preternatural talent with a football. And second the blankness of his public face, his apparent mundanity as a person. These two things play off one another. It's impossible not to feel some kind of personal connection to that talent, to feel yourself in the presence of something alluringly pure in the middle of all that heat and noise. For years it was tempting also to see something profound and telling in Messi's ordinary nature, the contrast of that extreme talent with the nerdish appearance, the mop of hair, the loping manner, the Andy Warhol-ish public statements, almost entirely devoid of meaning or interest.

Messi Business

Messi had something monk-like about him, an air of the holy sage. While other top footballers had tattoos and beards and golden-toasted highlights in their hair, Messi, the greatest of them all, looked beyond the vicissitudes of fashion, the genius as otherworldly man-child. Then Messi got some tattoos and grew a beard and had golden-toasted highlights put in his hair and was still brilliant, still performing on another plane, so that didn't really work out as a theory.

Against Iceland what was notable was the basic sadness of Messi as the game wore on. An astonishing statistic emerged. At the end of the first round of matches no outfield player had run less over ninety minutes than Messi. No outfield player had run less with the ball. Messi had run less even than Kasper Schmeichel and Hugo Lloris who are, of course, goalkeepers. In club football this has been bound up with Messi's success, a player for whom standing still, choosing his moments, creating space around himself have been a way both of saving energy and overcoming the press of opponents geared towards closing him down.

But he never stood a chance here. Watching Messi was painful at times. The Croatia game, Argentina's second group fixture, was the moment of crisis. I'd flown to St Petersburg to cover Brazil versus Costa Rica. It was a first sight for me of Russia's other capital. St Petersburg was built by Peter the Great to provide a Russian mimesis of European high culture and a grand seafaring port, the downside of which involved building on a huge marshland rife in summer with mosquitoes. The upside is a beautiful city, stone facades facing out into the Baltic with a lovely cool platinum light bouncing in off the water.

I was staying at the Park Inn, just out of town on a peninsula sticking into the Gulf of Finland. Dark brown, chunkily styled and placed at the end of a fountain-strewn Soviet piazza, it was the most unexpectedly vast hotel I'd ever seen, stretching down below ground level into a series of sub-caverns, then out along its wings into a network of closed-down swimming pools and lost conference centres.

After listening to the Brazilian manager Tite talk about Neymar for half an hour I got the bus back, packed a compass and a day's worth of food and water, and went for a walk around the Park Inn for the next few hours, scouting the foothills, exploring its north face. Finally it was time to eat a Classic New York Club Sandwich in one of the slightly sallow downstairs bars and settle in front of the big screen, surrounded by Brazilians, for Messi Part 2.

Argentina had made three changes for Croatia. Out went the scattergun Ángel Di María, the slightly stalled Lucas Biglia and the hair-raising Marcos Rojo. Javier Mascherano still commanded central midfield, a player whose tournament appearances to date resembled the harrowing final scenes of a notably gore-stained 1980s Vietnam war movie. At Brazil 2014 Mascherano had been a snarling, badgering force for order, his most notable moment ripping a hole in his own anus while performing a heroic match-saving slide tackle on Arjen Robben of the Netherlands. Four years on Mascherano had slowed but seemed if anything more prominent, another piece of furniture from the past in among all the ill-fitting, high-ceilinged talent.

Croatia had looked good in their 2–0 win against Nigeria in Kaliningrad, another team tied to an ageing crop of players, but with an urgency in their movements and in Luka Modrić a peerless playmaker. They almost scored in the opening minutes, Ivan Perišić racing down the left, cutting in and seeing Caballero pull off a fingertip parry. Around me in St Petersburg the Brazilians leapt up, hands on heads. There was a burst of laughter and high fives as Messi shot wide a few minutes later from a tricky angle.

And for a while Argentina continued to do what they'd done before, passing sideways across the pitch, a team playing hotel-lobby football, departure-lounge football, constantly waiting for something to happen. Or rather, someone.

With half an hour gone Croatia had begun to pull at the seams. Their manager Zlatko Dalić appeared on the touchline, a compelling, quietly spoken figure who would be a natural first choice if anyone ever needs to cast the movie role of Roger Federer's corrupt bank-manager cousin. Dalić had the right balance, his full-backs taking advantage of the space left by Argentina's sluggish midfield. Modrić was simply too good in the middle, always able to find those in-between spaces.

Chances started to come. Mario Mandžukić headed wide when it seemed easier to score. And by half-time a team of wonderful talents beyond its central player had continued to stumble, lost in the glare of that single dominating presence and with a manager too timid to fight against the process.

'We're at the point where Leo is untouchable,' Sampaoli had told *World Soccer* magazine before the World Cup. How can any team function in the shadow of this? Messi had touched the ball twenty times in the first half against Croatia. And with twelve minutes gone in the second half the game began to head one way, helped by another astonishing error from Caballero. Faced with a straightforward back-pass Caballero opted to float a delicately dinked ball out to Mercado. At least that was the idea. Instead the ball fell to Rebi, who smashed it back past him into the net.

In St Petersburg the Brazilians erupted. A middle-aged man in front of me spilt his drink, wrenching himself around to leap up and dance across the room. A close-up of Messi's face brought jeers and kisses blown at the big screen. He performed a slightly desperate slalom dribble. He moaned at the referee. And with ten minutes to go Modrić made it 2–0, sliding away from Nicolás Otamendi then spanking a drive into the corner.

Messi continued to mope on the fringes. Argentina's star substitutes appeared, Gonzalo Higuaín and Paulo Dybala, £200 million of attacking talent oddly hushed in the presence of their Jedi master. Finally Ivan Rakitić made it 3–0 in injury time. Croatia had been magnificent. Argentina looked inert. Messi ambled off without a word to anyone, having failed to register a shot on target and having made twenty-five passes all night.

Messi Business

Up in the gallery Maradona wept and held his head in his hands and had to be helped from his pew by his handlers. But as ever there was only one story in town. 'How can Messi make the team believe? How can the team believe in Messi?' asked *Clarion*, Argentina's biggest newspaper, not really offering any answers to either of these.

Five days later they beat a disappointingly blunt Nigeria 2–1 back in St Petersburg. Messi scored the first goal. It was a typically brilliant little miniature, taking Éver Banega's lovely pass in his stride and producing two perfect touches before shooting on the run across the teenager Francis Uzoho, who should have saved it. Again the response to Messi performing a moment of Messi was overblown and fawning, the mass forensic attention impossibly intense. The precision of his second touch on the run, killing the ball with a foot like an ostrich-feather cushion, was recycled and looped and gawped at on social media, crumbs from some holy relic.

Five days later Argentina were finally out, beaten 4–3 by France in Kazan in a gripping last-sixteen game they briefly led but never seemed likely to win. By then the collapse of Messi's last World Cup didn't feel as sad as it might have done. At the start of the tournament he seemed to be trying to play like the Messi of six years ago, to be the playground superstar again, winning matches from a standing start. It felt like a histrionic mini-drama within a drama, with the wider shared conviction that the World Cup needed Messi, that it couldn't flourish or succeed without its club-football superstars.

Unsurprisingly so. The star obsession in football has affected every surface, has created a strangely shrunken universe where individuals are judged on trophies hauled in and ranked on those relentless seasonal goal tallies. This has extended into the way we see the sport on television, with cinematic close-ups and emotive, cajoling cuts to the star players at every point of crisis. In Russia this gave us something else. We got instead the widescreen sadness of Messi, that great, wounded moon face, blank as ever, trapped within a prism of outlandish expectation.

This was always an unwinnable game. It is Messi's misfortune that only one player in football history has ever actually won this tournament on his own – and he was also Argentinian and also wore No. 10. But Maradona is the exception, the outlier, the fluke. One player does not lead his country to a World Cup win. Superstars do not alchemise base metal into gold.

This was the story once again for the would-be GOATs of Russia 2018. All of them struggled, from the sadness of Leo to the wretched theatricals of Neymar to the failure of Ronaldo to drag Portugal along under his arm. In many ways it was refreshing, a counter-narrative to the usual star fest and confirmation that international football remains a team sport, something that can't be swayed by status or money or spikes of individual genius. But which is still, defiantly, a matter for the collective.

5

We're On Our Way, We're On Our Way

24 June 2018

Sometimes everything just comes together. England haven't had many days down the decades where the cogs click, the runes align themselves, ripe melons drop about their feet, grapes crush themselves on their lips and suddenly everything just turns to gold. But they do come around sometimes, even at World Cups. And when they do, looking back, it's never really luck.

After the heat and noise of that opening win in Volgograd things had settled a little. The air had thinned out. The white noise had died back. Forget the second half. Ignore the streaky, late-breaking nature of Harry Kane's winning goal, the memory of all those other tournament bruises.

By the next morning that late-breaking victory looked like something else. Under Fabio Capello and Roy

Hodgson England's last four tournament openers had been drawn, lost, drawn and drawn, each one a shared sneeze of contagious anxiety.

This time around there was finally a little oxygen to breathe, space to stretch into. So this is how it feels to be a functioning tournament team, to be running ahead of the surf for once. All England had to do now to reach the knock-out stages was travel to Nizhny Novgorod and beat 'a style of hat', as Scott Murray put it on the *Guardian* Sport website.

Panama had reached their first World Cup by finishing above Haiti and Jamaica in their first qualifying group. After that they dead-batted their way to third in the second stage group, largely thanks to a mildly amusing implosion from the USA.

And in many ways the Panamanians were an inspiration, stuffed with street players and unlikely lads forced to travel abroad for league experience. Their presence at their first World Cup was a testament to team play and the enduringly robust romance of the sport. But they were also terrible, and terrible in the classic CONCACAF style, the most spoiling, bruisingly physical confederation of all the spoiling, bruisingly physical federations.

For now the tournament dynamics were in England's favour. With Belgium swatting Panama aside in Sochi the same night that England beat Tunisia, Group G had already fallen into two halves. A win in Nizhny Novgorod would present England with the luxury of working out how to 'game' their final fixture, resting players and toying with the benefits of finishing either first or second in the group.

We're On Our Way, We're On Our Way

The only real notes of tension that week were some strange noises off. Gareth Southgate dislocated his shoulder going for a jog, something that seems, frankly, impossible. He was treated by England's medical staff and appeared before the media in Repino with his arm in a sling, looking loveably rueful and goofy.

Of more concern was a slightly confusing story about England coach Steve Holland's training notes, which had been papped by a photographer on full display during an open training session at Spartak Zelenogorsk's stadium. For a day or two this was fanned into an inane sub-story. On the one hand the snivelling warthogs of the popular press had once again sabotaged England's World Cup campaign. Or something like that. On the other it was a harmless non-event. According to the 'team' leaked by the pic Raheem Sterling would be dropped for Marcus Rashford (he wouldn't be), Dele Alli was injured (who knew?) and Steve Holland was surprisingly neat with a blue ballpoint pen. All of which was no doubt powerful ammunition for the Panamanian intelligence machine.

Otherwise this all felt quite new, reporting instead on progress and stability and warm relations. Sensing the way this was going, mapping out territory others would follow, one national newspaper ran an article headlined 'How Gareth Southgate Became an Unstoppable Style Icon'. An otherwise illuminating fashion dissection, it also diluted its own argument by referencing José Mourinho, who these days strides up and down the touchline like a semi-retired neo-Nazi PE teacher who's spent the last three weeks sleeping in his car.

How Football (Nearly) Came Home

It was time to move on again. Following sport around is a very good way of seeing the world while only seeing very small, highly specific parts of the world. I've been to Munich enough times to get to know and love one bratwurst stall in the airport, one café just around the corner from the Mercure Hotel in the Old Town that does a good schnitzel, one Bavarian restaurant where the traditionally attired waiters look, dress and act like a frightening early twentieth-century militia group, and every single bit of the metro journey from the Marienplatz to the Allianz Arena. Otherwise, well, not a clue.

The Russian World Cup was about something else. It was about airports. There were plenty of contenders out there when it came to favourites. The day before England versus Panama I was in St Petersburg for Brazil and Costa Rica, which meant another snaking cab ride back to the impressive Pulkovo International with its enormous banks of bolted seats, its tiers of cafés and restaurants, its confusing elevator superstructure.

Samara was space-age in parts and agreeably 'throwback' in others. Moscow had three airports, Sheremetyevo, Domodedovo and The Other One, all of them huge, all miles from anywhere behind the endless scrolling horror of the Moscow ring-road traffic.

For me though, Clive, Nizhny Novgorod's Strigino International Airport was number one. Airy, high ceilinged and styled in light, uplifting greys and beiges, the Strigino delivered on every front. The entrance hall was large and airy but not showy, screens clear and prominent and, crucially, not exclusively in Chinese. Upstairs there was a secret hidden tier with beanbags laid out in front of the huge glass window. Best of all, the showstopper, it's so small you can walk straight out and into a bus into town at the kerb still feeling airport-ish and glamorous and a bit like the Beatles arriving in New York. Maybe one day all small-to-medium regional airports will be like Nizhny Novgorod Strigino.

This time around the concourse was thronging with England fans. It was ludicrously hot outside, heat that makes you want to stop and say OK, but seriously, what's the actual, how's the, when does it, this can't be. Still wrapped in my St Petersburg anorak and jeans I waited for a bit and smoked a cigarette and exchanged gossip about not much with the men from the *Independent*, envious as ever of the *Indy*'s rat-pack vibe, its hip young sports-writing crew.

I was staying in town at the Hotel Grand Business, which despite falling short of the high expectations generated by its excellent name, turned out to be a cheerful place in the leafy outskirts of downtown. As the sun went down I headed off into the old town and had dinner in a very cheap Russo-Italian restaurant with Andrew Roth, the *Guardian*'s Moscow correspondent. Next to us a table of Russians were watching Germany struggle against Sweden in Sochi on an internet feed streaming slightly ahead of the one on our phones. The sudden cheers and shouts and thrills as Germany struggled were capped by a spume of Russian expletives. 'Fucking Germans,' one of them shrugged, for our benefit. And so we learnt, ten seconds ahead of time, about Toni Kroos's sensational last-ditch winning goal. You see: Russians. Just like us.

Nizhny Novgorod is a sleepy kind of town. Until 1990 it was a 'closed city' dominated by the military, one of the centres where the Soviet Union developed its nuclear programme, with visitors strictly regulated. It still has a slightly thin, under-built feel. The metro rushes along gamely down its single track, upgraded with an extra dog leg across the water for the World Cup. The following day it ferried me down in the throbbing midday heat to the Nizhny Novgorod Arena for what already felt like an England flag day.

Gareth had brushed away the week's only other minor ripple, a nag from the press about the heat. Panama had travelled a day earlier and trained at 3 pm, peak sweat-soaking mid-afternoon kick-off time. There was a slight unease, programmed as we were by years of fudge and murky planning to spot these structural cracks. But Gareth, as ever, had a process. It made more sense to train early in the day, recover then travel, giving the body maximum time to be ready for the game. No drama. Trust Gareth. England are good at this now. One day at a time we were getting used to this strange, entirely unaccustomed feeling of the steady hand.

The stadium is a lovely light open white bowl laid out like a tambourine on its side in the middle of a spacious flatland on the edge of town. In a fit of high-summer sadism large glass panels had been installed around the upper tier below the roof, allowing the golden spires of the church at the top of the hill to peep in, but also slow-baking the England fans high up in the bleachers to a crispy finish as the day wore on.

England had made one change from the Tunisia game, Dele Alli sitting out with the thigh injury he'd tried to run off in the second half in Volgograd. Ruben Loftus-Cheek came in. Panama put out the same team that had been shrugged aside by a half-speed Belgium. Barrel-chested, all in red and quivering a little as they gripped each other by the shoulders, the Panama players looked close to tears during their magnificently full-throated anthem, a reminder of what just being here in the first place meant.

There was a reminder in the first minute too, as Gómez kicked things off by slamming the point of his elbow into Jesse Lingard's face near the far touchline. Panama probed vaguely but fell to pieces whenever they got anywhere near goal, swallowed up by the meaty rump of England's three-man defence, at times a back six as the wing-backs pressed in and Henderson dropped deep. For once at a tournament England's centre-backs looked calm, unstricken by any terrible anxieties, romping about the pitch entirely unafraid. Southgate had selected his defenders for their ease on the ball and their ability to fit the more studied rhythms of international football. This seems so unarguably sound it's a marvel no England manager in recent memory, outside perhaps Bobby Robson at Italia 90 and Terry Venables at Euro 96, has ever done the same.

And it was England's defenders who took this game

away from Panama in the first half. With eight minutes gone John Stones headed the opener. Panama had already made it clear that if they were going down they weren't going down without a series of aggressively insistent full-body hugs. It was the colonial British who had brought football to Panama in the first place. The men who built the Panama Canal included Bajans and Jamaicans who played football and cricket and planted the seed. Fitting perhaps that their descendants chose to turn up here and pay their own homage by performing like a bunch of notoriously angry Evo-Stik Premier League bruisers from a market town somewhere just off the A237.

Even before the opening goal the referee had to re-set England's corner twice as Gómez took a long, deep drink of Harry Maguire, wrapping his arms around that huge square chest, pressing his nose into his neck. And there was something comical about Stones's header, as both Maguire and Harry Kane were wrestled to the ground simultaneously in front of him, collapsing in a slow arc like a pair of power-station chimneys in a 1970s tea-time TV news report. England's players had already begun to shout for a penalty, two penalties, as the ball floated across to Stones, who planted it with thrilling power past Penedo's dive and into the corner.

Behind the goal the England fans bounced and rolled and fell over each other. England now had three goals at Russia 2018, all three from corners, and football had rarely felt so much fun. As Panama began to thrash around a little desperately they got another, this time from the penalty spot. Lingard was having a wonderful game, all shimmying movement, traumatising the right side of the Panama defence. Cutting inside again he veered on to Henderson's flighted pass and was bundled over by Escobar as he paused to shoot.

Panama yelled and griped and pawed at the referee. As Kane waited to take the kick Penado decided to lean on his goalpost in an attitude of cartoon insouciance. Kane waited, then spanked it into the top corner. In an odd aside Panama then tried to take a quick kick-off as England were celebrating, all ten red shirts haring forward and getting as far as Jordan Pickford's goal before the referee finally intervened to remind them this wasn't an Under-11s game on Tooting Common.

And by now England were moving in perfect time, one of those passages where every pass finds its rhythm, the ball pinged and eased around with a kind of hive mind, a flicker of the collective will.

Ten minutes later Lingard scored a beauty to make it three. Grooving in off the left he slipped the ball to Sterling, who laid it back into a huge open pocket of space on the edge of the area. Lingard just kept on running, took a touch and flighted the most outrageous dipping shot over Penea into the far corner, a move and finish so frictionless Panama were basically rendered invisible spectators at their own World Cup game.

I was pleased for Sterling, who had as ever been questioned, dissected, diced and filleted in the build-up to this game. At his pre-match press conference Gareth had politely fended off a series of questions from a Chinese journalist about the 'ridiculous' errors committed by England's footballers in the past, with specific focus on Sterling.

No surprise there. Nobody else has been assailed quite so relentlessly. It has been a difficult road at times on the pitch. Sterling has still scored just twice for England, against Lithuania and Estonia, and hadn't scored at all for more than three years. He has been a frustrating presence at times and even in Russia was more energetic worker bee than destroyer.

But there is something else here too. Nobody else felt Iceland quite like Sterling. For two years England's most talented wide midfielder had been abused and chivvied and harried for little more than the crime of being Raheem. Certain newspapers kept up the sneering coverage of the detail of his daily life, from references to fancy cars, to his domestic arrangements, to liberal use of racially loaded words like 'bling' to describe – God help us – the kitchen sink in the house he'd bought for his mum.

On the eve of this World Cup there was another clutching of the pearls over a new tattoo on his leg. The tattoo was of a machine gun, part of a tribute to his late father who was killed when Sterling was a child. Predictably there was a ludicrously censorious response, from daytime TV-show pundits to newspapers to the idiot-wind of social media, tinged as ever with some leering suggestion of feral black youth gone wild.

The odd thing here is that Sterling is a model professional and all-round nice guy. He works relentlessly hard, studies the game and has learnt at Pep Guardiola's knee. He's a role model. And yet, we get this.

After that Iceland game at the Euros I'd written an article suggesting this treatment was tinged with an unsavoury malice, not to mention veiled – or even non-veiled – racism. I remember stopping my rented Citroën at L'Arche motorway services en route to Lille for Belgium versus Slovakia, checking my phone as I ferried an unspeakable French burger to the plastic table and seeing I'd received a personal record five hundred tweets in about ten minutes, the majority of them in agreement, quite a lot of the others angry anonymous people ranting about Brexit and pant-wetting *Guardian* liberal quinoa-fondling enemies of the true Nordic caste.

Other, more influential voices objected. It died back for a while. Requests were made by Sterling's agent and an unhappiness expressed at the tone of the coverage. It didn't stop, though. His cars, holiday and domestic arrangements were all still up for grabs. Finally before Manchester City's home game against Tottenham in December 2017 Sterling was the object of an aggravated racist attack by a van driver called Karl Anderson outside the entrance to the Etihad Stadium. Anderson's girlfriend had asked him to wait and get Sterling's autograph. Sterling had happily obliged. At which point Anderson attacked him. Sterling was kicked and racially abused. He shook himself off, went inside, played 90 minutes and scored twice in a 4–1 win. It is a great shame that Sterling has to show this degree of fortitude and magnanimity, just as it would be no shame in the circumstances if he didn't.

Later in this World Cup there would be an acreage of words written about the multicultural nature of this team, its healing presence, its dreamily inclusive message about the 'nature of modern Britain' (all of these messages positive messages, happy messages). There is something in this. But only so much.

Back at the Nizhny Novgorod Arena England continued to play though a haze of sunlight. With five minutes to go to half-time they were 4–0 up, Stones scoring again from another worked routine. Trippier nudged the ball to Henderson, who clipped it to the back post, where Kane headed it back across the six-yard box. Sterling's header was saved. Stones butted the rebound gleefully into the roof of the net.

And yes, 4–0 before half-time is good. But it's not 5–0, is it? Not yet anyway. Three minutes later England had a second penalty after another outbreak of deludedly unsubtle manhandling in the box. Godoy dragged Kane down, the ref pointed to the spot, Escobar was booked for screaming in his face and Kane spanked the kick into the same spot he'd spanked the first. For the first time in their 68-year World Cup history England had scored five goals and done so in only half a game. This was giddy, dreamy stuff. In the stands the banks of England fans danced and fried in the sun and kept on singing that football was coming home, witnesses, two thousand miles from home, to a flag day in England's sporting history.

And yes it was only Panama. But it was also only England. 'There's a perception that England have always been hugely successful. When you dig deeper our history is actually different.' This was Gareth before the tournament. And it remains one of the great paradoxes of England's football history. Not just why aren't we better, but why do we think we should be? There is no hard evidence to support any sense of unfairly thwarted destiny. Rather than threatening to bestride the world, England have instead been relentlessly baffled by it. The issue of 'abroad', its otherness, its refusal to lie down or give ground or know its place has been the central note of confusion in England's largely non-illustrious footballing history. It took twenty years and a world war for the idea of actually playing in a World Cup to seem just about acceptable.

The first really lasting shock came in 1953 with defeat at Wembley to the great Hungary team of Ferenc Puskás, a moment of future-shock so profound the FA immediately realised something must be done. Jimmy Hogan, the former English footballer turned roving super-coach in the rapidly evolving central European scene, the father of the conquering Magyars, godfather of West Germany's great advances, was invited to give a coaching masterclass in touch and technique to a gathering of English coaches. Hogan was lined up to take on the role of the nation's technical director. Except, the FA changed its mind and carried along down another path altogether, one that would lead to the garden-shed bad science of Direct Football theory and to the lost decade of the 1970s, to renewed disappointments and fallings short, to the dwindling of the last few years. England came to this World Cup with six knockout wins at major tournaments of any kind since 1966. One World Cup semi-final in fifty years was a negligible return for a nation of such resources, such obsession. To the extent you start to wonder how deeply the obsession is bound up in the failure. This time. More than any other time. This time. This time.

Except this time was actually a little different. Yes, it was only Panama. But England had played terrible teams before and never scored five goals against them, had instead often struggled and puffed and become a strange, sweating, sullen version of themselves. A 5–0 lead at half-time was already the most impressive tournament result in England history. More than that it just felt like something different. Eighteen minutes into a lukewarm, post-adrenal second half it was 6–0 to England as Harry Kane completed his hat-trick with a goal that was both absurdly streaky and absurdly well constructed.

There were twenty-five passes in the move that led to the goal, the twenty-fifth Ruben Loftus-Cheek's scuffed shot that ballooned up off Kane's heel, floated down out of the sky and gently rippled the net. Kane had a hat-trick, England's first at a tournament since Gary Lineker against Poland in 1986.

There was still time for a nice moment. England had basically stopped playing after their sixth goal, following orders not to pick up cards or strain themselves unduly. And twelve minutes before the end Baloy made a different kind of history, scoring Panama's first-ever World Cup goal, to scenes of wild shared joy.

We're On Our Way, We're On Our Way

As the referee blew the final whistle Kyle Walker snatched up the match ball and punted it high into the red and white seats behind Jordan Pickford's goal. The England fans waved and laughed and sang in the sun, a moving, rolling block of flags and damp pink flesh.

'I didn't particularly like the performance,' Gareth said afterwards. 'Well, I didn't like the start, and I didn't like the goal at the end, but I guess the bits in the middle were pretty good.'

Although it didn't really matter what he said from here as something had shifted. Back in England the temperature was 34°C. The World Cup still had three weeks left to run. And for a moment in the middle of another fraught, dutiful, angsty English summer, when so many other parts of life seemed to be turning sallow and toxic, this felt like a moment of release. England were fun, likeable and charming. And Nizhny Novgorod was just the start. From here England were up, out there, floating in their tin can high above the earth. We had lift-off.

6

FIFA: The Men Who
Sold the World

2 December 2010

I can remember exactly where I was when Russia was
announced as the host of the 2018 World Cup. It was
2 December 2010. I was at FIFA HQ in Zurich sitting in a
padded auditorium chair staring idly at the back of Zinedine
Zidane's amazingly smooth and toned bald head, admiring
the contours and angles of his skull, the gleam of his skin
under the house lights. Zurich was the climax of three years
of politicking, bid-hustle and vast expense on all sides. Bid-
decision day had finally arrived. England were in the hat
with Russia, Belgium–Netherlands and Portugal–Spain as
contenders for 2018. Zidane was in the other side of the
draw, part of the Qatar bid team for 2022.

As an aside, I can confirm that he really does have a great
bald head, the bald head you'd expect from an über-athlete

of his status. Zidane has a head that would only be diminished by the intrusion of hair, a head to make you question in turn the basic validity of non-bald heads. Oh yes. It's a pretty good bald head.

This wasn't simply gawping at the megastar, although it was in part gawping at the megastar. From our row of press seats in FIFA's presentation hall you had to crane past Zidane and the rest of the Qatar delegation just to catch a glimpse of two other smooth, round objects of desire on the central stage. The World Cup trophy was present, coiled on its slinky black plinth. And next to it was the smooth round golden-toasted president himself, Sepp Blatter, on stage in his own purpose-built house of death to announce the results of both bids.

Zidane's head barely flinched as the word 'Russia' was read out, offering no more than a quizzical flare of the ear muscles. Five minutes later he was swept up onto his feet in a wave of leaping, bellowing men as the word 'Qatar' emerged from the second envelope. Zidane stood off to one side smiling a little awkwardly as his fellow ambassadors walloped each other on the back and punched the air. Beyond him Blatter gazed out across the rows of seats with an oddly strangled look on his face, the look of a man – and this was striking at the time – a little alarmed, for the first time, about what had happened here.

For the last twenty minutes FIFA's president had put on an extraordinary performance. Blatter was seventy-four years old, thirty-five years a FIFA executive and the last twelve as Lord of All Football. Towards the end of his time as FIFA kingpin Blatter didn't just covet and revere and worship the World Cup. With his shiny gold perma-tan, his bronzed head, his dinky little feet, he looked like the World Cup too.

Upstairs at FIFA House he'd writhed and pranced on stage in an uncomfortably sensual display, at one point literally smooching and nuzzling the trophy, drawing its gleaming golden orb close to his cheek in a gesture of mutual frottage. For the president this was a kind of coronation. But it would also turn out to be something else, the first act in the fall of the House of Blatter.

The FIFA building is an extraordinary place in its own right. Designed by the Swiss architect Tilla Theus, it has been described as an inverted skyscraper. This is a nice way of putting it. What kind of person builds a huge upside-down matt-black cave-lair into the side of a Swiss hill? On the third underground level, sealed within an aluminium hull, is the committee meeting chamber, designed as an impenetrable bunker. 'Places where people make decisions should only contain indirect light,' Blatter once explained. 'The light should come from the people themselves who are assembled there.' Well, it's certainly a point of view.

The endgame to all this is a part of football lore by now. Of twenty FIFA executives who voted on 2 December to award Russia its World Cup only one, Hany Abo Rida of Egypt, is still on the FIFA Council. Ten have either been indicted or banned from football. Five are suspended or under investigation. The Belgian FIFA delegate Michel D'Hooghe has successfully denied being given a valuable painting by Russian officials to swing his vote. Jacques Anoma of the Ivory Coast has successfully denied accepting bribes up to $1.5 million to vote for Qatar. Vitaly Mutko, once of FIFA and previously Russia's deputy prime minister, has so far successfully denied being the father of Russia's state-sponsored doping programme, which he also denied ever existed in the first place. Blatter has been banned from any future involvement in football for eight years over an agreement to make a 'dishonest payment' to Michel Platini, the ex-president of UEFA, who is also banned. The Argentine FIFA committee member Julio Grondona died in 2014 and, safely dead, has since been blame-loaded with successive misdeeds by FIFA itself.

Jack Warner of Trinidad has been called the greatest ticket racketeer in the world. Warner has been accused of embezzling pretty much everything he could get his hands on, including Haitian earthquake-relief funds. Senior US FIFA rep Chuck Blazer flipped, became an FBI informant, then died, leaving behind not just an ugly mess but tales of his own $6,000-a-month flat in Trump Tower to house his collection of cats, all paid for by CONCACAF funds. Blazer was eventually arrested for tax fraud while travelling on his mobility scooter to a fancy Manhattan restaurant.

Those who know FIFA best have often suggested Blatter wasn't the source of that darkness, but was simply its unseeing overlord. For Blatter football was never really about financial gain, beyond the president's salary and gluttonous perks. It was instead about power and ultimacy, the thrill of dispensing the favours of the world's most obsessively coveted travelling spectacle.

You could see the truth of this on stage. Before turning to his envelopes Blatter had spoken for what felt like at least six weeks, addressing his audience in rambling, gnomic sentences, at times seeming to forget what he was saying or simply stopping for a bit.

It was, to be fair, a room worth working. Bill Clinton had ambled in at the start arm in arm with Prince William. David Beckham was down near the front, waistcoated and glossed and groomed, like an impossibly handsome badger running a vital errand for the president of the space federation. Near the back Roman Abramovich smiled vaguely to himself, the smile of a man who never saw a sealed mystery envelope he didn't feel fairly relaxed about at least a few days in advance.

By the end Blatter had begun to look a little shaky. 'In football we learn to win and this is easy. In football we also learn to lose and this is not so easy,' he proclaimed as the room dissolved and people scuttled for the exits, phones clamped to their ears. And for a while Russia got a bit lost in all this. Right there and then the story was FIFA, English humiliation and the catastrophic wipe-out of the FA's bid. Russia seemed a footnote, the other guys. And looking back, this was part of the same process as the collapse of the bid, the basic solipsism of English football. Of course Russia won. This is FIFA. Had we not been watching?

Eight years later FIFA had moved on, swapping an autocratic bald Swiss for a bald Swiss autocrat in the shape of

Gianni Infantino. The governing body's World Cup HQ in Moscow was just across the river from our flat on Novy Arbat. The Radisson Royal Hotel is a huge, square-boned fantasy castle in the Stalin-does-Disney style. It was built as one of the Seven Sisters, intended to show the world the magnificence of high Soviet construction, and the tallest hotel in the world when it opened in 1957. These days it has its own fleet of river yachts and a forecourt clogged with outer cordons, inner cordons, handlers, spotters, soldiers, police, semi-soldier police types, men in sleek, black luxury saloons scanning the crowds and, most sinister of all, English-language news-wire journalists looking for a colour intro to their eight-hundred-word update on the power struggle in the South American federations.

Throughout the tournament the Royal loomed across the river at us, a statement of pure FIFA-power and of the natural fit between host nation and sporting body. In Moscow high-ranking officials have sirens to get them through the traffic. Wealthy Muscovites have been known to hire ambulances to drive in front of them to clear the road. FIFA had its own on-call motorcade, a train of sirens and thrilling black shiny sedans we would see going back and forth over the river through to the wee hours.

Coming back from the Panama game there was a sense of some point of tension having passed. Getting out of Nizhny Novgorod had been smooth enough. Breakfast at the Hotel Grand Business had looked at first like one of those sad, alarming occasions where you wander from hot plate to cold plate making calculations on what might be the least terrible thing to cram into your mouth. But never underestimate a Russian buffet. I had a cream-cheese sandwich, a hard-boiled egg and some cucumber and it was delicious, fine, nutritious, decent, right up until the moment over-confidence set in. Never eat the sausages. Everyone knows that.

And so it was back to the familiar comforts of the capital and a feeling of general relief. The last four England tournaments had revolved around some early-exit drama, either actual or feared. Not this time. England and Belgium would meet in Kaliningrad five days later to play off for the right to finish top, or second-top of Group G. Before that there was a World Cup to watch.

The same day England trounced Panama, Colombia had beaten Poland 3–0 in Kazan, James Rodríguez playing with the freedom of a man on a de-mob summer release from the rigidities of club football. In Samara Uruguay introduced a cold draught of sporting reality by swatting Russia aside 3–0. Saudi Arabia beat Egypt 2–1 in one of those brilliant World Cup games that mean absolutely nothing, have no bearing on the group, but which just seem to ride on their own gloriously fevered energy. Salem Al-Dawsari scored the winner in the ninety-fifth minute, volleying past Essam El-Hadary, who at 45 years and 161 days had become the oldest player ever at a World Cup.

In Kaliningrad Spain drew 2–2 with Morocco, Iago Aspas scoring the equaliser right at the end with a pirouette and a flick of his instep to ensure Spain topped Group B. Referee Ravshan Irmatov had initially disallowed the goal before re-allowing it after a video review. 'VAR is bullshit,' Nordin Amrabat, the Moroccan winger, had mouthed into the TV cameras as the players walked off. But it's more than just that. Above all VAR is the will of FIFA, Gianni's baby. And the Aspas goal was just one of an early slew of VAR-tinged matches, a new kind of televised drama conjured up with the referee striding over to his screen, possibilities and projections see-sawing wildly as a VAR decision altered the flow of an entire campaign.

And suddenly the World Cup was rocking along, its cogs and wheels turning perfectly, driven on by the the perfect fit between the grand dictatorial power struc-tures of Russia and the grand dictatorial power structures of FIFA. Plenty of nations have used the World Cup to placate the people, to build soft power, to legitimise a regime. For this tournament Putin scrubbed the cities, presented a face, ensured that we saw what he wanted us to. It was an exceptional piece of stage management, will-ingly absorbed and enjoyed by those present, including this writer.

But this was hardly a surprise. The World Cup has always been a circus. This is an event that has, like FIFA, always been heading away from its purest self. Jules Rimet was thirty-one years old when he helped found FIFA in a back room off the rue Saint-Honoré in Paris in 1904. Born in eastern France not far from the Swiss border, Rimet was the son of a grocer, a muscular Christian with a belief in sport as a force for egalitarianism. I like to think of the young Rimet as similar to the character of Potts in Evelyn Waugh's

Decline and Fall, one of those earnest young Europhiles of the 1920s with a belief in federalism and peace and ties across the industrial world. FIFA's founding members were France, Belgium, Denmark, Holland, Sweden, Switzerland and Spain. The German FA sent a telegram that same afternoon saying it was interested.

FIFA's first act was to help stage and co-ordinate the 1908 Olympic tournament, but the First World War almost killed the new organisation. Rimet went off to fight in the French army. The British home nations withdrew, unwilling to compete against wartime enemies. went off to fight returned from the war, became president in 1919 and FIFA survived on its subscription fees. It was at the 1928 Olympics in Amsterdam that the great leap forward came, as the idea for a World Cup was conceived and then staged two years later in Uruguay. Rimet travelled with the players by steamship carrying the trophy in his hand luggage. As moments of Year Zero optimism go, with the idea still out there of football and the World Cup as a purely sporting thing, an ideal of collectivism, this is about as good as it gets.

It took four years for Rimet's idea to be co-opted by Benito Mussolini. The 1934 World Cup was successfully hijacked as a propaganda tool for Italian fascism. Mussolini was obsessed with the sport's power as a mass intoxicant. His chief spin doctor Achille Starace, inventor of the fascist salute, was given free rein to stage Italy's World Cup. Fascist iconography defined the tournament's feel and look, which was intended to show Italy's despotic power but also its soft side, its vibrant good health, the happiness of its people. And yes, this did sound a little bit familiar in the summer of 2018.

This was not an isolated spike. Adolf Hitler was energetically trying to woo the 1942 trophy away from Brazil when the Second World War broke out. In the event the young men of Germany were busy pushing the Red Army back towards Stalingrad when the tournament was due to be staged and Germany 42 remains the great fascist World Cup that got away. Ever since dictators have courted FIFA. In 1978 the murderous Argentinian military junta was allowed to stage football's family-friendly beano. The final was held within listening distance of one of its most notorious police holding pens, where it is said some of those imprisoned were encouraged to cheer the sound of goals from the national stadium through their own black torture hoods. At that World Cup the German team was visited at its base in Córdoba by the Nazi Hans-Ulrich Rudel, a favourite of Hitler who fled to South America after the war, and from there helped assorted Nazi war criminals find sanctuary, including Josef Mengele, the infamous SS doctor at Auschwitz. Rudel had since worked as an arms dealer, neo-Nazi politician and adviser to Augusto Pinochet. All of which does put the fury over the presence of Sepp Blatter in Russia into some kind of context.

In terms of modern, hip, up-to-date corruption, the real gear change comes from Brazil. João Havelange, FIFA president from 1974 to 1998, is best seen as the godfather of modern sporting corruption. Havelange it was who signed the first mega-contracts with commercial giants. Along with his son-in-law Ricardo Teixeira he was eventually named in a 2012 Swiss prosecutor's report alleging a personal skim of $41 million on FIFA marketing-rights deals. Teixeira, a FIFA executive and chairman of the Brazilian FA, takes the biscuit here, a one-man embodiment of Brazil's culture of oligarchical corruption. In 2009 he was convicted of smuggling goods through Brazilian customs on the World Cup squad's private jet after its victory at USA 94. Teixeira had arranged that the team could go straight through, their baggage un-taxed. Rumour has it that Branco took an entire fitted kitchen back with him and Teixeira had the fixtures and fittings for a bar he opened a few months later. When the Swiss prosecutors finally caught up with him Teixeira skipped the country to Miami 'for health reasons'. The legal process is still circling. To date Teixeira has not been convicted of any crimes.

And so on to Russia and a World Cup that ran like an aggressively oiled machine, and where president and president seemed unusually close. This is a nation that defies normal categories, which is not a democracy, is not transparent, is not exactly a tyrannical regime either. But which is corrupt, cynical, alluring, gangsterish and deeply divisive. One thing quickly became clear from any Russia-based interaction on social media: you can't trust anyone's view on Russia. It demands a fixed position. If you say perhaps Russia should encourage a system of greater political opposition you will be accused of mainstream-media Russophobia in the pay of the great delusional global conspiracy. If you say Moscow is a nice modern city or that Russians are perhaps a little more open to the tangles and flaws in their system, you will be accused being a Putin-bot homophobe in the pay of the great delusional global conspiracy.

But then Putin's leadership in Putin's Russia is something different: a kind of non-hereditary plain-sight Tsardom. Putin has both a government and a court. Political opposition is tolerated, but also in effect sponsored and licensed by the Kremlin. Useful liberals are allowed to critique and challenge, a Punch and Judy without any punch. The writer Peter Pomerantsev called the system a 'a post-modern dictatorship'.

Russia has never been the same as us. Russians have experienced three transformative shocks on their own soil in the last hundred years: a revolution, a genocidal war and the fall of communism. That's quite a lot of shocks. And Russians like Putin. He gives them circuses. They are aware of this. The trappings of Western life are mocked as they're mimicked. The snapline for the shiny, fun, relentless TV network TNT is 'Feel Our Love'. TNT is sponsored by the state energy company Gazprom, the single largest carbon-guzzling energy company in the world. Gazprom has an aggressive stranglehold over European gas supplies. It's a tool of soft power for the Kremlin. And 'Feel Our Love' is, if you think about it, another really good Russian joke.

None of this is so different from FIFA, which is a source of power and an accessory to the most generous governments, not a force for peace, equality and votes for all, however it may occasionally present itself. It is the enduring paradox of football that even under all this irradiating heat, out there as the greatest corporate entertainment spectacle on earth to be bought and sold by everyone from global brands to despotic politicians, the game still seems to present something pure, a simple sporting beauty. Not to mention golden eggs so robust that even an organisation as grubby and inane as FIFA has failed to make any impression on its good health.

The night before the World Cup Final David Hytner and I made our way inside the Radisson Royal, past the lobby control, up two elevator rides, past Club FIFA, through the mildly horrified stares of the ladies who guard its entrance, and up to the fine air of the thirty-first-floor Mercedes Bar. From here Moscow rolled away in every direction, a supercity panorama. Wandering around each walnut-panelled corner, scoping out the marbled bar, we kept expecting to bump into Gianni, Vitaly, maybe even Sepp. But we settled instead for some shady types with sunglasses on and a very large Chinese man in a Simpsons T-shirt.

The next day Vlad and Gianni would appear together again at the Luzhniki. Once again Putin was entirely inscrutable, a small, utterly controlled figure. Infantino seemed a little frazzled and wild, repeating his mantra that Russia 2018 had produced the greatest World Cup ever. It is an extraordinary claim given the genesis of this tournament, the mud, the murk, the meltdown of FIFA's entire executive tier in its wake. Even more extraordinary, it was probably also true.

7

The Phoney War

28 June 2018

'We are not interested in the possibilities of defeat. They do not exist.'

This is the usual run of things in sport. Not least in football where first is first, second is last, third is nothing and fourth is probably Spurs or Chelsea. But there are times when the possibility of defeat can be just as interesting. Queen Victoria was writing about the Boer War when she urged the Earl of Balfour to focus his thoughts entirely on victory. Some might say England's progress from group stage to the knockout rounds of Russia 2018 was a matter of slightly lesser national concern. But there were moments in late June and early July when, frankly, you could have called it either way.

The thrashing of Panama had flicked a switch. Through the build-up and all the way to Russia there had been something restrained about England's World Cup, a fixation above all with keeping 'the expectation level' as low as possible. The merest hint of hope or praise would be furiously shushed on social media.

Until now that is. Panama changed everything. Suddenly it was on, the weather changed completely by that strangely frictionless 6–1 win in Nizhny Novgorod. By the final whistle the throttle had begun to rev, the glass to rattle. England had, it turned out, only gone and blown the bloody doors off.

The headlines next day were familiar and entirely expected. DARE TO DREAM. WE BELIEVE. ENGLAND MADE OUR LIONHEARTS ROAR. SKIPPER KANE CONVINCED ENGLAND CAN CONQUER THE WORLD. And of course DIANA DEATH RIDDLE AS BRITAIN SIZZLES IN SUPERFOOD SCARE.

For the first time pictures began to emerge of people back home watching England in public spaces, the tumbling, gleeful crowds that would come to mark the summer. A thousand people in Benidorm singing 'God Save the Queen' around a swimming pool. Men and women in replica shirts dancing wildly in some city centre to Offenbach's 'Galop Infernal', also known as 'the can-can music'. There were tales around the country of people leaping on top of cars, of spontaneous outdoor discos. Sam Allardyce was pictured eating a burger and watching the game in a pub. Suddenly the idea of throwing beer in the air seemed to have taken hold, each England goal greeted by a golden waterfall of draught lager, beer-soaked men hugging each other like gleeful sunburnt toddlers and singing that, yes, football was coming home.

There was a temptation to recoil from all this. England had beaten arguably the worst team they'd ever played at an international tournament. But to raise an eyebrow at early-summer English triumphalism is to misunderstand it. Most of the time 'It's Coming Home' was meant as an in-joke, a way of pretending that this boiling, sweating summer of escapism might never come to an end. And why not? Never mind football, life in general has been anything but straightforward, easy or drenched in sunlit hope the last few years. Britain has been a divided, slightly toxic place, wrung out by economic flatlining, austerity and divisive politics. Young people in particular have been told repeatedly and with absolute certainty that their lives are hard, stretched, pinched, that wealth is hoarded elsewhere, that things are shrinking, that there are too many wanting too little, that their carbon footprint is too big, that they can't buy a house, that they're weak and lily-livered and snowflake-ish, or alternatively under-educated, unwanted, a disappointment on a generational scale. Even their football was crap.

Well, here was something that felt a little different, an endlessly sweltering summer and in Russia an England team that played with energy and that had done more than those that went before, not less. Why not enjoy it? Throw that beer in the air. Hug your mates. Sing about things coming home. For a while, maybe just a few days, England's World Cup felt free and fun and like something else entirely.

There was just one thing, though. The group-stage end-game had turned out to be unexpectedly complex, with results elsewhere altering the nature of the draw. It now seemed likely that whichever team lost in Kaliningrad and thereby finished second in Group G would face a softer-looking path towards the final, with Spain the only really A-list name in that half of the draw. The nation that won and topped Group G would probably play one of Senegal or Colombia. But the winners of that game would then travel to Kazan to play Brazil, followed by the spectre of France in the semis.

And so the strategists began to strategise. From a desperation to win at all costs and a tearful response to finally seeing this happen, England were faced with something else. Better perhaps to contemplate the possibilities of defeat in Kaliningrad. Second place would sneak England into the weaker half of the draw. Plus of course the chance to rest players should always be taken.

The purists were shocked. A team selection with anything other than a win in mind could risk the dreaded 'loss of momentum', not to mention disrespecting the basic ideals of the competition. Positions were taken and energetically argued. My own view was that England should try as hard as possible to win every game because they haven't won that many games recently and winning games is kind of the whole point.

What's more, playing Brazil at a World Cup should be a life goal for everyone involved, not something to be shirked or avoided. In the end life is simply a series of moments, so choose the best of them, old boy, as I remarked while puffing on my ivory-inlaid pipe from the deep-brown Chesterfield of the colonial travellers' lounge at Moscow Sheremetyevo, or possibly while eating paprika Pringles and drinking a Dr Pepper on a bolted plastic stool next to the toilets by the Aeroflot queue – one or the other.

The variables of who and when and how would change once again before kick-off. Before then, it was time to luxuriate for a day or two in the oddity of the situation. For the last sixty-eight years of tournament football England had riffed through the full repertoire of ways to make their own life as hard as possible, from penalties, to meltdowns against the minnows, to not being good enough. As routes to tournament self-destruction go, beating Belgium to top their group was at least novel territory.

And so we headed off to wherever Matchday 3 might lead. Kaliningrad is a curious place, an enclave just a bit smaller than Wales that shares no actual border with the rest of Russia, but which instead sits between Poland and Lithuania on the shores of the Baltic. Kaliningrad was once Königsberg and part of Germany. It was seized in 1945 as the map blurred and the Red Army rolled across Europe. Eventually the tide rolled east again, but Königsberg was renamed and never returned, retained instead as a strategic port looking north-west to Scandinavia. For many years it was a slightly seedy place. In his excellent book, *Nothing Is True and Everything Is Possible*, Peter Pomerantsev notes that after the dissolution of the Soviet Union and its retention by Russia, Kaliningrad became notorious in the EU for offering its border nations some unique imports, specifically arms-dealing, narcotics, drug dealing, AIDS and a 'mutant strain of polio'. After the flies of Volgograd and the obscurity of Nizhny Novgorod, you did wonder a little about England's strategic placement at this World Cup. Sometimes it's almost as if someone's trying to tell you something.

The flight from Moscow took two and a half hours, the journey eased by the appearance of one of Aeroflot's remarkable 'meat-style' sandwiches. Old Kaliningrad has had some new money poured into its docks. Out by the stadium it remains nice enough but a little frayed at the edges, the air clogged with the smell of fresh diesel along its gridlocked two-lane highways. Like every other Russian city I saw there were green corners. In Kaliningrad a local man told me some older citizens still call their city parks 'Nixons', after President Nixon, whose visit to the Soviet Union in 1974 sparked a panic of city-wide makeover. Nixon, who never actually showed up in Kaliningrad, was gone from politics within the year, but happily his Nixons are still there.

Checking in at the large, grey, swelteringly hot Hotel Tourist I was pleased to note the sign indicating the ground-level late-night karaoke bar. The *Guardian*'s sport news correspondent Martha Kelner, a Hotel Tourist veteran, had issued a warning about this. Luckily I'd gone to painstaking lengths to find a set of wax earplugs, which I'd then very carefully left in my room at the flat in Moscow, so no problems there. I found a nearby Russo-Italian pizza restaurant hidden in a concrete cube behind a small wooded area up the street. Best of all, Senegal versus Colombia, a game with particular relevance to England, was on the telly. Although even this would start to feel a little problematic as the evening wore on.

It had been a gripping, occasionally startling end to the group stages. The night before I'd been at the Spartak Stadium for Brazil versus Serbia, but it was the early kick-off that had provided the shock of the opening round. Crammed into the tiny, sweaty Spartak media centre I'd stood around the banks of TVs with an assortment of English journalists watching Germany struggle against South Korea. In the opening week I'd been at the Luzhniki to see Jogi Löw's team run into the ground by Mexico and listened to Löw sound utterly baffled afterwards. A week later, with Sweden beating Mexico in Yekaterinburg, defeat could mean the world champions went out at the first hurdle.

As ever Germany kept the ball relentlessly, but they just seemed to be tickling away at the face of the game. Kim Young-gwon and Son Heung-min both scored in injury time as the match sagged and became strange, with Manuel Neuer up in the South Korea box and the Spartak media centre transformed into a melting pot of delighted global citizens, cheering wildly as the goals flashed in. Most vocal of all were the gathered Brazilians preparing for their own nation's final group game, although any ideas of significant revenge at Russia 2018 for the horrors of 2014, 7–1 and all that, would be short-lived.

How Football (Nearly) Came Home

The complications weren't quite finished in Kaliningrad. By kick-off it would become clear that Group H had resolved itself a little differently. Against expectations Japan had hijacked second spot, nudged ahead of Senegal by their FIFA Fair Play ranking. Colombia finished top. As a result the winner of England's group would now play Japan in the last sixteen while the runners-up got Colombia. There was a significant difference here. Japan were ranked six places below Panama. Colombia were sixteenth in the world and quarter-finalists from four years ago. The reward for victory in Kaliningrad would now be an easier tie on paper. Too late though for England or Belgium, whose teams had been picked, their tactics set. This would just have to play itself out.

*

And so in a city that isn't really in Russia England and Belgium played out a World Cup group-stage decider that wasn't really a decider, but was instead a fudge, a bluff, a waiting game. It was at least another lovely summer evening in the north. The Kaliningrad Stadium is a medium-sized white bowl surrounded by the usual wasteland of walkways and fences and broadcast compounds, with a series of levels picked out around its exterior, making the whole thing look like a very glamorous, white-panelled, out-of-town car park.

As the sun dipped below the lip of the stadium roof the grass had a mossy, marshy-green quality, different from the more parched-looking Nizhny Novgorod. In the stands both sets of fans sang and cheered happily before kick-off, but with no real sense of tension, more an air of generalised celebration. It all felt a little unreal, a little dizzy and light, not so much tournament football as a pause for breath.

I'd walked in through the England fans on the stadium approach and been struck again by how dogged and game that travelling throng had been throughout this World Cup, finding their way through the most muddled of paths to the most distant of queues on the wrong side of town at the end of a triple-layover flight. Russia was fun to visit in many ways and easy to enjoy. But these middle-aged, everyday people had spent thousands of pounds getting here, had booked time and holidays, and suspended their weekly grind months in advance. And now here they were, watching a scratch England team shadow box at an international tournament.

In my section of the press seats there was a slight bafflement over how to report this, how to tell the story in a way that made the occasion feel suitably grand given the fanfare, the coverage, the sheer expense of the whole thing. Belgium had made nine changes, England eight. Pickford and Stones remained at the back and Loftus-Cheek in midfield. Beyond that Phil Jones and Gary Cahill came into defence, with Trent Alexander-Arnold making his competitive England debut in an actual live World Cup game. Danny Rose was on the left. Eric Dier and Fabian Delph would provide the midfield hustle. Up front Marcus Rashford and Jamie Vardy played as a pacey, slightly odd-couple front two, the academy princeling paired with Kenickie from *Grease*.

How Football (Nearly) Came Home

It was at least a chance to see Vardy start at a World Cup, a player I've loved watching in the Premier League for his maniacal energy, his playground style, his air of triumphant outsiderdom. When Vardy scores he still celebrates like it's all a glorious heist or a mugging, scooting off to the corner like a dog with a string of sausages in its mouth. In between he mainly just does the same thing over and over again, an agreeably pared-back game-plan that basically involves running in behind, looking for space, time and the angle to shoot.

Plus of course, he has that unique Vardy status in this modern England team. Increasingly, as the tournament wore on, England's players were required to mean something, their success required to have some broader purpose. The players were seen as part of a culture shift. England's fans could identify with them, could feel an empathy and a connection. At least, more so than with the previous sullen, entitled superstars, remote behind their golden sheen.

This is a slightly problematic idea. Being a professional footballer is a more remote profession now than it ever has been, even for those who exist below the very A-list or have risen through the levels. In this slightly mixed England group the majority were still top-tier academy kids who have lived the professional life from childhood, removed from the park and school teams, the amateur game, anything resembling most people's experience of football. Younger England players such as Loftus-Cheek will have been VIP-laned from the start, cloistered away in the parallel world of world-class facilities, informed nutrition and elite-standard club pitches.

The Arsenal player Joe Willock has always seemed to me like the acme of this process. Willock was spotted aged four by scouts on the touchline of one of his brother's games and signed up to the youth system. He wrote in Arsenal's programme a few years back, when he was seventeen, that he had never played for any other team outside of Arsenal age-group levels, from park to school and up. His entire sporting life from age four has been lived on a professional sports pitch, behind the velvet rope, away from the harmful effects of the everyday.

It would be great if Joe Willock became a World Cup winner in 2022. But it wouldn't say a thing about 'English football' in the wider sense, about the grassroots, about the wider health of the nation, about participation and physical culture and the use of resources to benefit the many and nurture talent everywhere. Or in other words, all the social benefits a healthy national football team is supposed to indicate. Instead our football only skims the cream, is in effect a privatised, outsourced industry. Coach a team through the youth leagues and you'll notice the best players disappearing from six years old onwards, plucked out from the terrible pitches, the dad-coaches, the troublesome nutrition of park and recreational football. Their triumphs speak to this other world, the one behind the secret door, not to any wider sense of public benefit or municipal investment paying off. For all the excitements of Russia 2018 and the success every year of the Premier League, the parks and recs the rest of us use are still bogs in winter. The changing rooms have still been vandalised. Green space is still being blocked out.

Contrast this with the players who won the 1966 World Cup, who on the whole really did reflect and represent the people cheering them on in the most straightforward sporting way. These players were a product of something shared. Bobby Moore was someone you might have played with or against until he was signed by West Ham aged fifteen. Bobby Charlton was spotted playing for his school aged sixteen by Manchester United. Jackie was a miner for a while, then tried to join the police, then went into football full-time.

Vardy at least knows a life outside football. As a teenager he worked shifts in a factory making prosthetic limbs. He got into trouble. He skulked about the lower levels of football. Even as a pro he had his troubles coming up through the levels. At one point in the Championship he asked his Leicester manager if he could go back to Fleetwood Town because he didn't think he was good enough. For a while he self-medicated his injuries by dissolving different flavours of Skittles in a bottle of vodka then sitting in an armchair with his leg up drinking it. But he is at least a product of the same world, the same forces as the average English human, with the talent to leap onto the other side of the fence.

As the game kicked off Vardy's first act was to tear forward at the red-shirted defence and spank an overhit pass towards Rashford, all fizzing energy, heading, as ever, only one way. Otherwise England began a little sloppily. Youri Tielemans shot powerfully from twenty-five yards and drew a one-handed save from Jordan Pickford, palming the ball up in the air from just under the bar. A few minutes later Cahill cleared off the line after Pickford had let the ball squirm through his grasp. Otherwise it was room-temperature stuff, friendlier than a friendly, both teams shuttling the ball about carefully but without malice.

The sun had begun to fade by now, but the stands still had a holiday-ish air. And for quite a long time nothing happened. Really, nothing. England fretted a little. Belgium kept the ball. England stood in front of them like a defensive pawn structure in the most tedious game of chess ever played. As the clock passed forty-five minutes the referee Damir Skomina of Slovenia allowed five seconds of stoppage time, then whistled things to a merciful stop. There were even some cautious boos as the players walked off, which goes against the wider feel-good narrative but is nevertheless the truth. As things stood England would top Group G by dint of having accumulated fewer bookings.

This was a game that needed a goal, needed some kind of narrative simply to justify the occasion. It got one six minutes into the second half. It was an outstanding moment of skill in the middle of all that dross. From a standing start Adnan Januzaj jinked in from the right, produced a showy double-shoulder drop that lulled Danny Rose to sleep, then whipped a sensationally well-flighted shot into the top-left-hand corner of the England net. Thibaut Courtois would later suggest that he, Courtois, would have saved it because he was a bit taller. In reality this was just a brilliant goal, the ball hit so early and with so much overspin that it beat Pickford's clutching hand by an inch, then dipped down behind him as it bulged the net.

The stadium woke up with a shout. The celebrating Michy Batshuayi slammed the ball on the bounce back off the post and into his face, garnishing a brilliant goal with his own special tribute. And Belgium were away, their fans singing and bouncing on the far side, the better grooved, more coherent team, and now streaking away with the group come what may, Brazil be damned.

Januzaj is an interesting player and an interesting figure to decide this match. It's easy to forget that he was sounded out by Roy Hodgson for a possible England call-up in 2013, a little amateurishly as it turned out, given he didn't actually meet the qualification period. He'd been at Manchester United from the age of sixteen and qualified to play for Belgium, Serbia, Albania, Kosovo, Turkey and Croatia. Initially he refused a Belgium call-up while he weighed up whether to play for Albania, his father's country. Kaliningrad was his first goal for Belgium, arguably the high point of a career that has stalled and stuttered a little at times.

Januzaj. We knew, somehow, it was going to be Januzaj. My *Guardian* colleague Dominic Fifield had said before the game, yep, I bet he scores the winner, and that familiarity was striking in itself. It has been said that the Russian World Cup proved that the Premier League really could produce a world-class team of players. The only slight drawback: they were called Belgium and they play in red.

Kaliningrad was an incestuous game in many ways, with

twenty-three players on show who had played in or spent major parts of their youth in the Premier League. There was a wider story to the most Premier League World Cup match ever played, one that snakes back into England's own mixed and fraught international history. Winter breaks, bad luck, cheating foreigners and mental blocks be damned. In reality the separation of ownership and control of the England team has always been the single greatest reason for its failure.

From the foundation of the Football League in 1872 the clubs and the national association have been separate bodies with separate interests. There is no other major league in the world where this is the case. The league has been run for profit alone. The players have been disposable chattels, soaked, rinsed out, underdeveloped, easily replaced and now brought in from abroad, Meanwhile the FA has been left to wonder about things like player production, the national team, the system, joined-up coaching, a domestic production line.

There is no incentive for any English club to produce English players, to coach them properly, to give them time to develop. The FA can't insist on an overhaul of academies or pressure selection, as the German FA did in the aftermath of their own slump in 2002.

There have been moves to address this in recent years, a ramping up of academies, some much-trumpeted coaching cooperation with the FA. But the England team will remain trapped inside the limitations of its own domestic game, picking from the leftovers, asking for favours.

Does this matter? The Premier League can, with some justification, point to its competitive edge, the fact it benefits everyone not just England. Certainly Belgium are one of quite a few nations to profit hugely from its pathway out of the weaker domestic leagues. The balance in Nizhny Novgorod was on their side, with a far greater depth of Premier League experience in Belgium's squad. Eden Hazard and Kevin De Bruyne had been the best players in the last two Premier League-winning teams. Romelu Lukaku's move from Everton to Manchester United was most expensive domestic transfer of all time. Even the manager Roberto Martínez is basically one of ours, the intense, ferrety, occasionally quite funny manager of Wigan and Everton, and a man who will, whatever he achieves, always be associated with 4–3 wins, 3–2 losses, relegation, FA Cups and an agreeably intense touchline persona.

England did have their chance to level it in Kaliningrad. Vardy played a lovely pass through the inside-left channel for Rashford, who galloped in on goal and then hit a slightly weak curling shot that Courtois fingertipped around the post. Such was the confusion around those last knockings some would even suggest Rashford missed on purpose, was under instruction not to score. It is a genuinely absurd idea. There was time still for Marouane Fellaini to produce a magnificently horrible knee to the thigh of Loftus-Cheek. And that was pretty much that. Belgium topped the group and would face Japan. England would travel to Moscow to play Colombia at the tightly packed Spartak Stadium.

The lasting impression as the players applauded the

crowd was of a slight down after the highs, a World Cup game that was never really chased down with any feeling. Trust in Gareth, trust in the method. This was the new mantra. But England would now move into the knockout stage under the first real cloud of pressure, all of it self-induced, after deliberately weakening the team and losing their first match in ten months. Southgate had chosen a path. It was a ballsy move. The players would be rested. But for the first time Gareth now had something to lose in Russia.

'The knockout game is the biggest game for a decade,' he told the press room in Kaliningrad, accepting what was to come, owning, as England like to say, the situation. England would walk out against Colombia as narrow favourites, not least because by contrast José Pékerman couldn't rest James Rodríguez in the final group match against Senegal, ruling him out of the England game as his calf injury was aggravated. Either way Colombia in Moscow already felt like a jumping-off point, something quietly epic; not to mention, as it would turn out, the real beating heart of England's World Cup summer.

8

Spain, and Coming to the End of Things

1 July 2018

In between his more highfalutin literary work, John Updike wrote a series of brilliant comic stories about a fictional writer called Henry Bech. Author of a single career-defining Great Novel, Bech has since ossified into a literary celebrity, a silver-haired grandee following the fame circuit of conferences and fancy parties, doing what Philip Larkin described as 'going around pretending to be me'. All the while Bech remains utterly blocked, unable to complete another book to follow the magnum opus. Towards the end of the saga Updike has Bech holed up on a Caribbean island as part of another junket, this one a luxury holiday during which Bech is supposed to autograph thousands of copies of his reissued masterpiece. Wrist cramping, lost in all that endless repetition, the words 'Henry Bech' swimming in front of his eyes, by the end his impotence is total, his journey complete, his stasis terminal: the great author can no longer even write his own name.

As a set-up to a single punchline it's a pretty epic effort. It was also an image that sprang to mind at least once during Russia 2018 while watching the brilliant, transformative champion teams of the last two World Cups. In Moscow, Sochi and Kazan, Germany seemed to lose themselves in their own method, keeping the ball so long they almost forgot they had it, disappearing into their own style. Three days after England versus Belgium in Kaliningrad Spain did something similar in Moscow, producing a performance that was both absorbing and horribly painful, football reinterpreted as a terminal toothache.

There has been something brilliantly pure about Spain's interpretation of football over the last decade. This has involved taking one part of the game, the pass, and refining it above all others until it becomes too much for an opponent to handle. In Moscow at the start of July the most gilded national team of the modern age were knocked out of the Word Cup despite producing surely the most statistically dominant drawn game in the history of international football. In 120 minutes of football Spain had an astonishing 79 per cent possession. They made a mind-boggling 1,115 passes to Russia's 291. Overall Spain had the ball for ninety-five minutes at the Luzhniki Stadium, but still only managed nine shots at goal. It was an extraordinary kind of fudge, relentless high-class, high-grade football, just somehow without any real football in it.

How Football (Nearly) Came Home

By the end this slow-burn semi-football, the endless pass and move, felt almost too much for Spain's players and their stand-in manager. There they were yoked together by a style and a set of rhythms, embarking on an endless draining circuit of the Luzhniki Stadium pitch, ink running dry; and unable by the end to write their own name.

*

Before then there were loose ends to tie up, duties to discharge, planes to catch. England's final Group G game, the 1–0 defeat by Belgium, had ended with a trip to the mixed zone down in the concrete catacombs of the Kaliningrad Stadium. This is a big part of England duty, the chance to speak to the players, to squirrel away quotes to be used during the week, and to hang around in a dank grey tunnel being jostled by a Dutch TV crew.

The set-up is usually the same down here. The classic mixed zone features a row of metal barriers to create a winding channel from dressing-room door to players' exit. Pressed up against the railings various groups of media, TV, radio, daily and Sunday newspapers stake out their huddles and wait for the players to emerge carrying their wash bags and running for the safety of the team bus. Through this prism a controlled kind of exchange takes place, players hooked in or ushered over by prior agreement, the plaintiffs and beseechers periodically breaking off from their small talk to shout out things like, 'Jordan. Jordan. JORDAN. Jordan, MATE ... Oh well, fuck it.'

The big point about the mixed zone, the one thing all

newcomers must instantly grasp, is its strictly enforced etiquette. There is no written constitution. But convention is meticulously overseen, territorial waters powerfully controlled, personnel aggressively vetted. Everyone who's been in the zone for any length of time will have seen fists bunched, recorders batted away, outsiders berated for joining the wrong huddle. I've seen at least one English journalist swing a punch or two, defending the sanctity of the huddle in a corner of some foreign stadium corridor that will be forever England follow-up (Wednesday 10 pm embargo). But then, this is just the zone. It's a hot zone. It's a zone of tears, a zone of standing around occasionally shouting, 'Gianluigi! English press!'

On big nights there are three main types of people down here. Most important are the regulars, people who understand how this works, who approach it with the right level of informed professionalism, know the media officers, know when and who to arraign from the other side of the railings, and who basically make sure there are some quotes around to put in your daily newspaper.

Tagged on to these are the hangers-on, the occasionals, people like me. Attaching yourself to a pack of mixed-zone regulars you get those looks, friendly but a little pitying, like veteran platoon commanders in the Nang Delta being presented with some callow recruit straight off the boat and holding his gun backwards ('This is what they're sending us? Alright, kid, fall in').

Finally at World Cups you get the mixed-zone stars, the odd Big Name Broadcaster or Mega Hack, the TV face who clearly feels they're on the wrong side of the railings and who takes this chance to finally reach across, alpha to alpha, and say, 'Hi Jordan mate,' or 'Dele old bean,' or 'Diego! Un abrazo amigo!' At the last World Cup the American football journalist Grant Wahl did an insightful interview with a magazine where he mentioned dressing specifically to 'make an impression' in the mixed zone, describing in detail his bespoke denim jeans that he doesn't ever wash due to their precious nature, just occasionally freezing them overnight. And he's right. The appearance of a tall, dandyish-looking man in piss-stained frozen jeans is always likely to clear a decent space at the railings.

I managed to miss most of the Kaliningrad mixed zone having rushed down from Gareth's press conference, which felt extra poignant given the oddities of England's weakened team. But even down here there was a feeling of heightened intensity, of the chance to build towards something now with Colombia in the sights.

Getting out of Kaliningrad was difficult. The dinky airport was swamped with England fans heading in every direction, many taking complicated routes through Poland or Scandinavia. Some had chosen to drive, gunning the family saloon back through Germany and Belgium. The rest seemed to have washed up in the Italian restaurant in departures, where the staff basically gave up and sulked after the first five hours of people asking why the beer had run out, demanding pizza and going on extensively in song about It Coming Home.

It was good to be back in the capital after the clogged

arteries and cramped side streets of Kaliningrad. By now a city that had seemed alien and frighteningly large on that first night felt like home. I rode the metro back from the airport, impressed all over again by its magnificence. Stalin built his metro as another kind of folly, something grand and superman-scale to ennoble the (otherwise rather badgered) Soviet citizen. The metro was dug insistently deep, with marbled corridors, endlessly scrolling escalators and the feel in places of a vast Victorian parlour. One of its best features is the lack of posters and advertising, the sheer blank walls relieved only by the odd grudging sign telling you where you might, just about, be heading. There has long been a rumour of an even deeper metro, Metro B, the secret network built below the public one and reserved for party officials and persons of influence. Metro B can be found only via various secret entrances, from where it leads to a giant bunker for use during enemy attack. If it sounds too far-fetched and paranoid to be true, it's also far-fetched and paranoid enough to be completely plausible.

*

With the group stage over we had two days to draw breath, to chuck the rotting food out of the bottom of the fridge, to remember to Skype home and to re-scatter around the country for the start of the knockout stage. Moscow chose this moment to become grey and sombre and drenched with sudden squalls of drizzle. I went down with a kind of sweating sneezing bug that had been doing the rounds, and which made it necessary to camp out all day watching the rain inside the coffee shop just up the road from our flat.

Spain would play Russia in Moscow on Sunday 1 July, an occasion I'd been quietly drooling over ever since it was announced. The first round of knockout games was the day before. This would be the moment the World Cup really changed gear, with two genuinely gripping games from Kazan and Sochi. First France beat Argentina 4–3 at the Kazan Arena on an afternoon marked by some fine, occasionally wild attacking play, and the spectacle of two divergent superstars. Kylian Mbappé scored twice and produced a jaw-dropping sprint from his own half that brought a penalty to open the scoring in the 13th minute. Everyone knew about Mbappé, had known about him since his emergence as a gilded teenager at Monaco through to the mega-move last year to Paris Saint-Germain. But this was the moment he really announced himself as a player ready to gambol across the grandest stage in the most rarified company. It was also the moment Lionel Messi's World Cup met its promised end.

Messi didn't play badly at all. But he looked like the Messi of Russia, moping through an otherwise frantic ninety minutes with that air of stillness, of something strangled and mournful, a man who seemed to be at the other end heading towards last things and exits. On Novy Arbat there were cheers from the lines of passers-by watching the restaurant TV screens as France progressed and the day faded into Portugal versus Uruguay in Sochi, another delicious-looking knockout tie. Edinson Cavani, the world's most absurdly handsome footballer, decided it with two fine goals. Pepe's equaliser for Portugal made him their oldest-ever World Cup scorer, a record that had also been broken at this tournament by Cristiano Ronaldo and the ageing urchin Ricardo Quaresma, the moral of which is that, just maybe, your national team might be getting on a bit.

And so it was finally time to see Spain at the Luzhniki. This was a game that would either see the hosts go out or the most influential national team of the last decade reach what already felt like a kind of end point for many of the players. And maybe even – some would have it – a system, a way of thinking about the game.

Spain had suffered already at this World Cup. The entire process of preparation had essentially been junked by the revelation that Juan Lopetegui had secretly betrayed the federation to take the Real Madrid job. Lopetegui had been appointed after the last Euros. Spain were unbeaten in twenty-two games under him. They'd thrashed Argentina 6–1 in March, beaten Italy easily in the qualifiers, scored five against Costa Rica and seemed to be finding an edge, a blend of speed and power to go with that grooved keep-ball style. All of which fell to pieces two days before the tournament. Mayhem ensued.

The chairman of the Spanish FA Luis Rubiales had received a text message alerting him minutes before Madrid made the announcement on its own social media channels. Spitting with fury, Rubiales flew to meet Lopetegui on the next plane, ignored the pleadings of members of his squad and immediately sacked his manager. Fernando Hierro stepped up as caretaker, not long after ruling out ever taking the job. Spain had plodded through the group stages, intermittently bright and captivating when Isco and Andrés Iniesta found their elegant little patterns, at other times an ageing team of technicians, a little stuck in their own grand ball-playing traditions. They were still among the favourites. They still looked utterly vulnerable. And on a gloomy, rainy, muggy day in Moscow there was a feeling of something brewing in the air as the host nation prepared for its own first World Cup knockout game since the Soviet days of 1986 and that epic 4–3 defeat by Belgium – Igor Belanov, Vasily Rats and all that.

The good news was Sid Lowe was in town for this game. Good news, first because it's always great fun to spend time with Sid, the *Guardian*'s Spanish football correspondent. And second because he knows absolutely everything about Spanish football, has watched and written about this current generation at least as much as anyone else I can think of, and simply watching Spain with Sid has its own kind of galvanising energy. The only problem was, he appeared to have turned up in a kind of pre-zombie state, arriving at the flat on the morning of the game having not slept the night before, hot-foot from a late one in Sochi with Portugal and Uruguay. Sneezing, shivering, popping Russian painkillers, I woke Sid up from an unscheduled doze over his laptop. We staggered out into the rain for a quick, half-eaten burger from the hipster place up the road ('distinctive Russian burger with gold leaf') en route to what would be one of the most engrossing, draining, unforgettable days of the tournament.

To say central Moscow was gripped with World Cup fever would be to push the definition of the word 'fever' beyond the mildest of flu-like symptoms. The cafés and bars of Novy Arbat were not filled with flags. The air was un-rent with cheers, the pavements free of face-painted children. Travelling to the Luzhniki three hours before kick-off it was hard to know when the train had actually arrived at Sportivnaya, so entirely void of booming nationalistic chants was the half-empty carriage.

But then, Russians don't really do public euphoria in quite that way, for all their quietly fevered nationalism. Russia-love comes out in other ways, is more a deeply held conviction, a burden to discharge. Like America Russia seems to feel the need not just to succeed, but to mean something, to assert its stoical will, to be, in some vast and painful sense, the land of the chosen people.

Lenin wrote about this. Russian super-nationalism was a threat to the true creed of Bolshevism. Worshipping personality was an obstacle to the collective. This desire to tear down the old idols didn't work out as Lenin might have hoped. There are currently eighty-two statues of him around Moscow, including the one that rises up in front of the grandstand at the Luzhniki. There he is, looking off to one side with an air of destiny, eyes fixed on some glorious collective future, all the while tactfully ignoring the words 'Official Fan Store' plonked just below his feet; and beyond this the row of fancy stalls for soft-drink giants, luxury cars, electronics manufacturers and the largest commercial yoghurt-drink supplier in China.

As Sid and I headed for stands loaded with water, caffeine, paracetamol and vending-machine chocolate the team sheets began to circulate, with some significant changes on both sides. The playmaker Alan Dzagoev had recovered from injury but would start on the bench next to Denis Cheryshev, a more puzzling omission given his status as Russia's best creative player.

There was of course a back story here. On the eve of the game Cheryshev had been forced to deny publicly at the pre-match press conference that he had used what may or may not have been a banned substance. The suggestion this might have happened came from an interview with his father Dmitri in *Sport Weekend* magazine, picked up by journalists seven months later. Cheryshev junior was out of the Russian squad at the time.

'He received an injury and, because of the miscommunication of doctors, they began to inject him with growth hormone,' Cheryshev senior said. Cheryshev junior later denied this. The Russian Football Union also denied it. The RFU maintains Cheryshev's words had been 'incorrectly interpreted' by the journalist interviewing him. The player has never failed a drugs test.

But the story had grumbled away in the background before resurfacing in earnest in the build-up to this game. The Russian federation had been opaque in response. Cheryshev impossible to pin down. Nobody was available to respond or take their right of reply. It would probably have disappeared had Cheryshev not, by chance, been put up to speak to the media at the pre-match press conference. Immediately he was pounced on by those present who had been following the story and asked to confirm or deny its veracity. At which point, Denis, you've become the news.

Russia had shifted to three centre-halves for this game and packed their team with glowering energy, ready for the long haul. Russia's running stats were already the marvel of the World Cup, with more yards covered than any other nation, tribute to the invigorating effects of a little home-town nationalism mainlined right into the arteries. Spain had left out Iniesta and brought in Marco Asensio, a runner for an artist. Diego Costa would play up front, Koke in mid-field. The inferior being currently impersonating David de Gea would continue in goal. Beyond that, this was Spain at their most muscled-up, ready for a ninth attempt at finally beating a host nation at major tournaments, an eight-game losing run that stretches all the way back to Italy in 1934 and takes in losing to England on (God help us) penalties in 1996.

*

The Luzhniki was full, its steeply banked sides crackling with a genuine fervour as Russia kicked off. At which point the game fell instantly into its pre-set pattern, ball, players and referee all sliding off down towards the Russian goal en masse, like a match being played on the deck of a sinking ship. Necks craned that way as Isco and Jordi Alba and Koke shuttled the ball around in between midfield and attack. The pressure was constant but diffuse, like a red-shirted weather front. And already the crowd had started to whistle as the ball began its long, arduous, lonely journey from Spain to Spain and back to Spain over the next 120 minutes.

Russia sat back and waited, an extraordinarily disciplined, cussed, hard-headed display of non-football. For Russia this was foot without the ball. For long periods it was simply standing in certain preordained areas while some other people kicked a ball nearby. It was in its own way quietly magnificent, led from the front by the gloriously ungainly Artem Dzyuba, so tall, so angrily present in every clinch and grapple, like a street-fighting scarecrow, chin unshaven, trousers held up with a pin.

There is an overwhelmingly tangled set of theories on why Russia aren't better at football, from geopolitical complications, to the well-paid complacency of the domestic league, to the fact that quite a lot of people prefer ice hockey. The last few years hadn't helped. Sergei Ignashevich, who started this game, had also played against Spain in the semi-finals of Euro 2008, part of a Russian team that played with such a wonderful sense of freedom, only to atrophy over the last ten years, an emblem of Russia's own increased isolation.

Ignashevich it was who scored the opening goal at the Luzhniki with eleven minutes gone, albeit in the wrong net. There may be more horrendous sporting experiences than scoring an own goal at your home World Cup while lying on the floor being jabbed in the kidneys by Sergio Ramos in hyper-evil mode. But not many spring to mind. It was a horrible moment. Yuri Zhirkov had fouled Nacho out on the right. Asensio curled in the free-kick. In the middle Ignashevich tried something unwise, entering into a full-body wrestle with the King of Darkness. As both players fell the ball floated down out of the sky, struck Ignashevich on the heel and deflected into the net. Choose your battles, Sergei old boy. There is a time for trying to out-shithouse Sergio Ramos on a football pitch. And that time is never.

And so we settled down for another edition of death by a thousand short passes. There have been changes in personnel, but this Spain was still very much from the post-tiki-taka playbook: a possession team, dreamily good on the ball, crammed full of feather-footed technicians; but with the same vices too, the same tendency towards embroidery and stasis and passing for passing's sake.

At times playing this Spain team must have felt like being battered to death with a toothpick, like being eaten alive by gnats, like trying to run through a swamp in snow shoes, like being spectators at the world competitive knitting championships, like being forced to run fruitlessly from side to side while small, nimble, earnest men pass a ball around for an hour and a half.

Up in the stands I'd already started to sketch out an intro for a Spain win, for Vlad Agony as Sergio Boys Roll On. Spain had this. A goal up and in almost constant possession of the ball, constructing delicate little gossamer patterns. Sid wasn't so sure though, and Sid knows. He's followed this team and these players through the golden years, the most successful concentrated period of success achieved by any European team ever, not to mention the most transformative tactical methodology of the modern age.

I was also following Spain around at Euro 2008 when that team first began to click into gear. Funnily enough it was a 4–1 win against these same opponents that really announced the Spain Supremacy. There was summer lightning and rainstorms in the mountains above the Tivoli-Neu Stadium in Innsbruck that day as David Villa scored a hat-trick in a 4–1 win notable for Spain's unusual ease in possession, the way Xavi Hernández and Andrés Iniesta and David Villa, back in his sniping left-winger days, could keep the ball with such ease.

It seems telling that the UEFA stats page on that game doesn't record the split of possession, because people just didn't do that then. We hadn't been made to look. But this was the start of the possession age as Spain produced a kind of football not seen before, producing players of such refined technique that under the new rules dampening the impact of physical strength, contact and tackling, they seemed at times to be more or less unbeatable. This was a team that simply took the ball away from its opponents, not so much blowing them away as reducing them to frazzled, exhausted spectators at their own defeat. This came from the Cruyff legacy at Barcelona, a way of playing that made a fetish of passing and moving, relegating things like running power and aerial challenges and broken play to subsidiary elements. The influence of this style has been profound and all-pervasive, from the dad-coach shouting 'Don't send it' and 'Don't go long' at park level; to Germany's world champions, who exited the tournament in a blur of toothless keep-ball; to Gareth Southgate's own preoccupation with preserving energy by keeping the ball.

There is, of course, a limit to all things. Spain's possession game was driven to its remarkable absolute by the presence of a one-off genius of a passing midfielder in Xavi, the exception that made the style work in every context. Xavi dragged Spain into excesses at times, but still kept the wheels moving. In Russia the Spanish game tended to revolve around Isco, a beautiful footballer, for whom taking and passing and giving the ball looked like a sensual pleasure. In Spain there were those during this tournament who felt that Isco slowed the team down, that he was a rather earnest little soloist, adding trills and fills between the beats.

Plus opponents are wise to it now, less psychologically disturbed by sitting deep and watching. At times such as these possession of the ball can feel like a burden in itself, something stifling and onerous, denying your own attack space. Russia were behind at the Luzhniki, but they didn't change their game; they continued to let Spain pass themselves dry. With thirty-six minutes gone Dzyuba linked with Zobnin and set up Golovin for a shot just wide. The crowd didn't so much roar as wake up with a start. But it felt like a hint of a weakness behind the lure of Spain's passing mastery.

And five minutes later the Russians were level. Gerard Piqué leapt with his arm in the air and succeeded in punching away Dzyuba's flicked header. For all his wild gestures of innocence, his stunned expression, it had to be a penalty. Dzyuba rolled it into the corner and he was off in a veering arc, beating his chest, as around us the Luzhniki leapt and seethed and writhed. I sneezed for the fourteenth time since kick-off. Next to me Sid shrugged a little. He'd been right.

Did Spain hit back, shift gears, take a breath, pause, lift their game? No. They didn't do any of those things. They just kept on doing the same thing they'd been doing when they were doing the same thing as the thing they were doing before that.

Half-time arrived and passed in a daze, all sense of urgency bled away. From the top tier of the press seats you get a slightly giddy aerial view of the Luzhniki pitch, the perfect angle to follow the peculiarly turgid repetitions of those red shapes going through their patterns, the ball funnelled lovingly from left to right, lurking in pockets, turning backwards into space.

Do Spain ever get bored of their own style? Midway thought the second half, with their entire team set out in the Russian half, there was an astonishing spectacle as the Spain players simply pushed the ball back and forth across the defensive bridgehead. It seemed almost sarcastic, like a team falling in on itself. In part this was caution. Spain know what other teams want to do to them. They knew Russia were coiled for a counter-attack. So we have something similar to what chess players call 'zugzwang', a situation where one side doesn't want to move, where the only result of making a move is to open up a weakness, with safety only in stasis.

Which is all very well. But it's a migrainous spectacle at times. Not to mention lacking in thrust to create the overlaps, the sudden points of strength against a disorientated opponent that are the whole point of the passing game.

It is worth noting that this isn't some innate thing. In its earliest days the football played in Spain was a furious, wild thing. For a while coaches would place water troughs at the side of the pitch so that players could dunk their heads into them during the game and find some relief from the agony of running. As recently as the 1990s Spanish football was still known as a leg-chopping, butcher's delight. The keepball tradition is a recent one. But it has been all-pervasive, to the extent that what we saw at the Luzhniki felt a little debauched, a perversion of some true faith.

With a little over twenty minutes to go Andrés Iniesta appeared, thirty-four now and an employee of Vissel Kobe of Japan's J1 League. This was a little more pain in its own way. Iniesta is one of those pure pleasures, a player whose game is all craft and control, but also mischief and joy. Through his time at Barcelona and Spain he will always be synonymous with the best days of the Barca–Spain possession game. But his entire sporting personality is the opposite of the cold-custard football that was on show at the Luzhniki, the feeling of a team slowly eating itself.

Iniesta it was who made the last meaningful attempt to save us from the brain-ache of extra-time, drawing a fine, low save from Igor Akinfeev with five minutes to go. And so on we went into the extended march on the road to penalties. Towards the end of extra-time the delayed gratification, the needless tickling titillation, became almost unbearable. The home crowd had by now reached a state of constant excitement, aware that something strange was in the air here, that a weird kind of voodoo was hanging over this Spanish team. It felt as though these footballers were being made to live out an endless, oddly satirical version of themselves. Yes, Spain. Pass. Pass more. Bring it on. We know where this is heading.

You just knew who was going to win the shoot-out. When it comes to newspaper deadlines and penalties you generally tee up two intros, ready to send one or the other after the final kick is taken. As the rain continued to fall, as Russia's subs came out onto the touchline to gesture at the crowd and urge them to cheer louder, Spain continued to weave their patterns with an ever more melancholic air. I decided to just do a Russia one.

Full-time of extra-time brought a huge rolling cheer around the stadium. Perhaps the crowd knew too. Ramos won the toss and Spain elected to go first. Would they remember how to kick the ball forward? Iniesta stepped up and passed his penalty into the corner. Smolov, Piqué and Ignashevich all scored. Koke put his kick too close and too high and saw Akinfeev palm it away. Golovin scored, with de Gea once again absolutely nowhere near saving any of these. Cheryshev pinged one down the middle. Aspas marked his run, skipped in, shot straight and hard, but saw Akinfeev deflect the ball away with his heel as he fell to his right, the ball ballooning back even as he began to punch the air.

And so Russia had run and scragged their way into the quarter-finals, an unexpected but entirely deserved host-nation presence. Isco had touched the ball 198 times at the Luzhniki. Vladimir Granat came on and played the last seventy-five minutes for Russia and touched the ball just eleven times, completing zero – yes, zero – passes in that time.

On the Spanish side the temptation was there to see this as the endgame for a system and a way of playing. But Spain fell apart at this tournament before it even began. They were unlucky, out of time at the wrong time. And in Moscow they were on the wrong end of surely the most statistically impossible losing game ever played. Right up to the final weekend Spain had still made the most passes at the World Cup, despite exiting at the first knockout stage.

The debrief was long and tangled. On the concourses and corridors along the top tier of the Luzhniki, Russian people sang and hugged each other. A stream of badge-wearing media types hustled down to cram their way into the Luzhniki basement where Stanislav Cherchesov, Russia's manager, credited his own genius with the victory. 'I really had to persuade my players that this was the only way out,' Cherchesov said. 'We don't like this kind of structure but this is what we had to do with three defenders. Thank God my footballers understood what I was telling them. They trusted me.'

Putin hadn't been there for this one. Some said the

president couldn't risk being present for a defeat, that he was reluctant to associate himself with Russia exiting its own World Cup. Victory turned out to be a more attractive prospect. 'Just like the whole country, Putin watched the game from start to finish and cheered for our lads,' a Kremlin spokesman clarified. Dmitry Medvedev, Russia's prime minister, had attended the game. After the victory he published a picture of himself celebrating with the team. In the photo Medvedev and the players are with Vitaly Mutko, who you may know from such family favourites as the International Olympic Committee's Russian doping case, being banned for life from the Games, being in charge while the alleged state-sponsored Russian doping factory was going on and sitting on FIFA's executive right through the meltdown of the Blatter years. His presence at the moment of triumph was an eloquent statement in itself.

As evening faded into night I sat on the floor in the mixed zone waiting for Sid to finish his Spanish-speaking vigil and trying to stay awake. Eventually we left the stadium feeling stuffed with football. Spain's exit had been sustained and all-consuming. It felt all the more so as it played out once again on the huge TV screens on the pavement on Novy Arbat, where we ate a late-night steak as the sun started to peek in at the edge of the sky. At the halfway point in this World Cup thoughts would turn to England and Colombia two days from now just across town at the Spartak Stadium. It seemed reasonable to expect something a little less draining than the defeat of Spain. Incorrectly, as it would turn out.

9

Colombia, and the
End of All That

3 July 2018

Rademal Falcao has a graceful way of moving, as you might expect of someone nicknamed – when anyone remembers to call him it – El Tigre. Even after 120 minutes of being jounced and jostled by a heavily perspiring Harry Maguire, Falcao still has something glossy and feline, a sheen of star power as he walks from the centre-circle to the edge of the penalty box. It's twelve minutes before midnight in Moscow and the thing everyone secretly knew was always going to happen has indeed begun to happen.

It's a strange feeling witnessing a penalty shoot-out live in the stadium, with a sense of things running away from you, of too much information to process. This is how it feels watching from the press seats, which are so close to the pitch at the Spartak that we can hear the players' shouts even over the noise of a last-sixteen tie. Falcao still has that air of preternatural calm around him. But then this is a footballer who made his professional debut aged thirteen, who has played in six different countries, survived two potentially career-ending injuries, scored 256 goals, and is still here aged thirty-two, strolling up to take the first penalty like no one's watching.

Jordan Pickford bounces manically on his line. Falcao just stands and looks at him for a moment, then spanks the ball with startling power straight down the middle as Pickford dives off to his right. Later Pickford would say that Falcao's penalty was the only one that threw his pre-match planning, the only one that went the other way.

England are behind for the first time at this World Cup in a significant game, 1–0 down in a penalty shoot-out. The air seems to sag, to fill with some heavier substance. Harry Kane walks briskly, spots the ball, shimmies for a moment, feet battering the turf, then skips up and hits his penalty low and hard past the dive of David Ospina. The ball is struck so sweetly it clanks back off the bottom of the frame of the goal and flies up into the top of the net. England's players barely break ranks, or flinch, or celebrate in the centre-circle. They're not supposed to. This is part of the plan.

*

Three weeks into this World Cup there still weren't many England fans in Russia. In Kaliningrad Gareth Southgate had called the last-sixteen game against Colombia England's biggest for ten years. But only 2,225 made the trip in the end, officially anyway, and Moscow had been grey and grizzly and quiet in the build-up. Russia's defeat of Spain had been followed by a wild night in the capital. People swung from the street furniture. Cars blasted out Moscow hip-hop. The squares and boulevards were packed with booze, dancing, fun, disorder and various other things that might well usually be forbidden around here. Most of the time this World Cup did feel like a controlled environment, something calculated and carefully parcelled out. At others it felt like something more unplanned, with its own kind of heat, its own energy.

By the next morning the city was calm again. The long, thin park outside our block was staffed by its regular cast of head-scarfed babushka types eating breakfast rolls, just along from the shoeless drunks still asleep on their benches. But the England shirts stayed away still, the bubble of rising excitement back home only felt at one remove.

What you did notice after the Belgium game was the constant chat and chunter, expressed in part through an explosion of jokes, in-gags, funnies, clips, internet memes. Suddenly 'Football's Coming Home' was everywhere again but this time in an arch, often quite funny form. For three weeks in summer the combined creative will and technical expertise of the English people was poured into the making of humorous clips on Twitter. Naturally Hitler in his bunker in *Downfall* got the 'Three Lions' treatment. Footage of Vladimir Putin playing the piano was edited so he seemed to be happily rattling out the opening bars. The ear-chopping scene in *Reservoir Dogs* was re-cut as a paean to 'It's Coming

Home'. Somebody even did the 'Marseillaise' scene from *Casablanca*, the most stirring musical moment in any film, but re-set here over Alan Hansen saying, 'We'll go on getting bad results' and an alarmed Jimmy Hill suggesting, 'It's bad news for the English game'.

It was easy to miss if you took all the giddy triumphalism too seriously. But this was an unusually funny World Cup run, funny in a way no England tournament has ever been before. Overblown and slightly delirious at times, the self-referential jokes and snarky asides were all part of the running in-gag. It was hard not to think again of the shared gloom of recent years, and not just around England football. At moments like these, with the sun beating down from day to day, you got the feeling people just really did need something to laugh at.

With the knockout stages powering on Brazil eased past Mexico in Samara. More significant for England, Belgium beat Japan 3–2 in Rostov in a wonderfully topsy-turvy game that Japan had been leading 2–0 with an hour gone. It was a result that shifted the weather slightly. Gareth had made a call on this, preferring to rest players and take his chances with first or second in the group. Now Belgium had overpowered Japan, who might have played England had Kaliningrad gone differently. Whereas Colombia always looked like a game that would go right to the end.

Trust in Gareth. That week we heard for the first time about the detailed preparations England had been making for the looming trauma of a penalty shoot-out. It made sense. English football has tied itself in knots over the shoot-out. Five times in eight tournaments between 1990 and 2006 England had exited a tournament in this way. And still there were those who insisted this was bad luck or a curse or hoodoo or worst of all a losing ticket in a lottery.

Which, of course, it isn't. Scoring or saving a penalty kick is a test of technique, preparation and fortitude. Southgate knows this from close-up, because missing a penalty was the defining incident of his professional life. He'd written about it in his autobiography fifteen years ago, but he wasn't telling us a bad-luck story. The real story was a lack of knowledge, craft and prep. Andreas Köpke had read Southgate's unpractised movements, that gauche, upright run to the ball, the scuff down the middle.

And so on Southgate's watch England's players would be sent into battle properly armed. Since March his squad had been practising penalties, but also working on the details around a shoot-out. Kicks were taken at the end of training when the players were tired. Disruption techniques had been incorporated, players screaming at each other from the side as they took a kick. Psychometric tests had pointed to those best at handling pressure. The details were refined, from planning the way players walked from the centre-circle (quickly), to how to stand, how to react to a miss or a hit, and the absolute importance of choosing your spot and sticking to it. Untangling the variables, 'owning the situation'. This was the plan. And having a plan – any plan – was at least something new.

*

How Football (Nearly) Came Home

Next up for Colombia is Juan Cuadrado. Like Falcao, Cuadrado has also played the whole 120 minutes. He's thirty now and a champion with Juventus, his aborted spell in the Premier League a forgotten diversion. Cuadrado is tough, the product of an unimaginably hard childhood. He doesn't look bothered by any of this, stuttering like Kane at the end of his run, addressing the ball at an angle and spanking it hard and high into the corner. Pickford flails his arms around, frustrated at having chosen the right side and been beaten. But that ball was buried with feeling.

Marcus Rashford steps forward for England. Rashford is all talent, all promise, but also a twenty-year-old with one goal for his club since March. He walks up briskly then does that alarming thing, backing away in an arc to make his run-up, but approaching the ball with practised ease and striking it with such severity that it rips into the bottom-right corner of Ospina's net before he can get close. Rashford veers off on his way back so you think he's going to wave to the crowd. But he's actually going to Pickford, going with a hug and a hand clasp, a man who likes playing for Gareth and who likes playing for England. The score is 2–2. In the stadium around us people stand and hug themselves and hold their heads. But it doesn't feel like we're quite at the moment just yet.

*

The Spartak Stadium is a blue-collar kind of place, smaller than the Luzhniki, and home to Spartak Moscow, the city's trade-union team. The metro train up from central Moscow bounced alarmingly as it howled through the tunnel between its final stops, disconcerting the yellow-shirted Colombian hordes who had block-booked this game, packing out the walkways and verges on the way into the stadium. Back in England the heatwave was proving unbreakable. The game was a 7 pm kick-off on a hot, sunny Tuesday night, perfect for the World Cup economy of bars and pubs and closed town squares, the urge to gather together and consume this spectacle that already felt like it was running away on its own momentum.

Southgate picked the team he was always going to pick, the 1st XI from the Tunisia game. José Pékerman made one enforced change for Colombia, replacing the injured James Rodríguez with Jefferson Lerma. It is hard to overstate the importance of this, the absence even from the bench of a player of such craft, so driven by these World Cup games. Colombia were a good fit for England generally, a team of underachievers, given the country's size and the talent that has passed through those yellow shirts. The quarter-final defeat to Brazil four years ago was as good as it had ever got.

Colombia hadn't beaten England in five attempts. All five of those were against more illustrious England teams than this, a list of names that even now still conjured a sense of slight anxiety. It was hard not to feel that whatever happened here it would come down to the most minute of details, the last fingernail, the last breath.

It was dark by the time the teams walked out. The Spartak's narrow curved ends were a seething yellow block under the lights. At the far end the painted Saint George's

How Football (Nearly) Came Home

Cross flags had been staked out grimly, Luton, Stockport and Hull popping up in between the huge Colombian tricolours. Even the press seats felt surrounded, with a crush of friendly yellow-shirted fans on one side and the large Colombian media presence taking up the front rows.

There are some things that simply go against the grain in this business. Wearing accreditation in airports, for example. An English journalist will literally rip his badge off his neck the moment he leaves the stadium gate for fear of being branded a wanker-badged jobsworth. Any kind of pageantry or fan-dom or cheering your team is the main *bête noire*. Colombia are the chief rule-breakers on this front. At the last World Cup there were people in the media seats with painted faces and a Miss Colombia in full skimpy team colours in the media room. Moscow was more restrained, with just the one replica shirt in the press row in front of us. But there was something a little prickly in the air.

The Colombian national anthem filled the stadium, the final lines shouted from every corner. All business, unintimidated, I rearranged my twin caramel nougat bar and water-bottle collection. England were playing an away game here. And still you didn't fear for them or feel that familiar anxiety. Down in his dugout Gareth stood, jacket already off, the silky back of his waistcoat gleaming under the low Spartak lights. He seemed a strangely moving figure in his old-fashioned tailoring, hair swept to one side like a 1920s intellectual. As Colombia kicked off he turned and sat down just own row below us, and the stadium fell quiet just for a moment.

Colombia, and the End of All That

England stretched that silence out in the opening moments, pressing high and hard, winning the ball back and keeping it. For ten minutes Raheem Sterling had what would turn out to be his best sustained passage of the World Cup, sprinting into spaces down the side of the Colombian central defenders, forcing a foul from the towering Yerri Mina and throwing himself into that muscular Colombian shield. Mina was forced into one desperate handball. Moments later he ended up being piggybacked around in a near-perfect circle after he'd hurled himself on top of Sterling, draping himself across his shoulders like a giant bearskin coat. It is easy to overlook Sterling's strength on the ball at times. Mina is 6ft 5in. He ambles around the pitch like a treehouse on legs. At the start of this game Sterling threw him off balance with his powerful running, his fearlessness, his ability to bounce an opponent aside with that powerful rump.

Colombia dug in, fought back and began to drag their nails down the back of this game. England kept the ball and probed vaguely. But this was different to the group matches. This young team was being stretched and bruised in new ways, made to concentrate on every movement and also on the dialogue in between, the game of nudges and kicks and constant debate with the rather wired-looking officials. Ashley Young was England's appointed barrack-room lawyer, scuttling over to keep up his dialogue with the linesman at every heavy tackle, every push in the clinches.

There had been some pre-match concern about the American referee Mark Geiger, a maths teacher from New

Jersey and still *persona non grata* in Panama after a contentious performance during the Gold Cup semi-final against Mexico in 2015. Geiger was censured on all sides after a hasty red card and penalty award against Panama had decided the game. The next day the Panamanian newspaper *Critica* carried the memorable headline, '¡Fucking Arbitro!'

England still had the snap, the movement and the fizzed passes in those opening twenty minutes as Colombia sat deep and tackled hard. In the press seats we could bask in the novelty of seeing an England team whistled by South American opposition for having too much of the ball, for passing too carefully at the back.

The physical hustle was ceaseless. England ferreted after Colombia's playmaker Juan Quintero every time he got the ball. Quintero has the physique, the style and the indolent skills of another era, a player moving to a different set of rhythms. At one point, under all sorts of pressure, he played a perfect little pass through Henderson's legs to Juan Cuadrado, waiting for the space to open up then sliding it through with a cruel precision.

At the other end Sterling peeled off the left, beat two men and saw his shot blocked. This was the pattern: precision, followed by heavy traffic, and ending with a slight misstep. It was easy to forget at times that these England's players had spent much of the last few weeks waiting for these moments. Sterling had played 230 minutes of football, or fewer than three completed matches in the previous seven weeks. He hadn't scored a goal for anyone since

22 April. At the Spartak he kept finding the right space, just not necessarily at the right time, or with his body parts aligned the right way.

Kieran Trippier had begun to press with authority down the right. Kane either wrestled the last man or dropped deep and spun. Maguire and Cuadrado shoved each other by the touchline over a throw-in. Nobody threw themselves to the ground or waved a stricken arm at the officials. This was airless, breathless stuff.

Moments later there was the first proper, game-stopping melee as England paused over a free-kick close to goal, the red shirts infiltrating the Colombian wall and finding themselves energetically repulsed. In the middle of it all Henderson barged into Barrios, who dropped his head on to his chest then raised it up to nuzzle against Henderson's chin, a semi-butt that left Henderson collapsed and lying prone on the floor, victim of his own hitherto well-hidden super-fragile glass jaw.

Referee Geiger whirled his arms and frowned and consulted VAR and eventually decided only to book Barrios, presumably deciding his butt that was just about within the butt guidelines. A few minutes later Mina threw himself to the ground like a dying redwood, apparently knocked unconscious by a trailing arm from Sterling. Briefly, in stoppage time at the end of the first half, some football happened. Jesse Lingard leapt high to control a bouncing ball but lashed his shot over the bar from just inside the area. As the players wandered off at half-time they looked pumped up, eyes wide, shirts soaked with sweat, the air in the stadium pulled tight around them. And already something else had begun to lurk behind all this, an endgame that would insist on playing itself out.

*

Next up, Luis Muriel steps forward and simply rolls his kick into the corner, shifting his angle at the last second as Pickford goes right, an outrageously confident finish. Pickford would later suggest he picked Muriel's penalty. But he still dived the wrong way.

It's 3–2 to Colombia as Henderson walks forward, flicking up the ball into his hands halfway to the penalty spot. As he does this something starts to shift a little. You can feel it, almost like an urge to shout. He looks calm, but painfully calm, a man wearing his most ill-fitting calm face. Henderson has been an urgent, necessary presence in this England World Cup team, the one concession in the Southgate selection to a more familiar kind of England player, the cajoling presence. Henderson is a runner not a technician, a great team man and a player with just enough of that old pointing, shouting spirit. Much would be made of young players unscarred by tournament failures past. Henderson carried all those bruises. He was there in Kiev in 2012, in São Paulo and Manaus in 2014. He was in Nice for *Iceland: The Meltdown*. This is an act of will for him.

As he gets close to the penalty spot, waiting for David Ospina to step back onto his line, Henderson does something stomach-wrenchingly awful. He starts to do keep-ups with the ball. No, Jordan. This is not your unveiling at the

Bernabéu. We are not convinced. No matter how admirable, how undeniably ballsy it might seem in its own demented micro-moment, this is off-script. This is not a man nailing down every variable, owning his nervous ticks, sticking to the plan. He's going to miss, someone says nearby. Possibly it's me. And Henderson looks flat-footed as he stands there. The ball seems heavy suddenly, as though it will have to be dug out from under his feet. The kick is weak, side-footed, lacking in disguise. Ospina gets down low and saves. Colombia lead 3–2 and this is slipping the other way. Strangely though, and not without a sense of resistance. It isn't supposed to go this way. Not this time.

*

Half-time had brought another note of needle. ITV pictures showed a member of Colombia's backroom staff bumping into Sterling with his shoulder as the teams left the pitch, trying to draw a reaction, then marching over to the fourth official and complaining about dirty tricks on England's side.

The second half started the way the first had ended, a match stuck in third gear trying to accelerate up a hill. England's midfield didn't just look a little absent, or a little lacking in craft. It looked like an unfilled hole in the middle of all that movement. It was as though England were wearing themselves down as well as their opponents. At which point Colombia helped them out. With fifty-three minutes gone Young hit another hard, flat corner from the right. Carlos Sánchez headed it powerfully away. And suddenly

England had a penalty. Sánchez had been called out for grappling Kane under the ball, a finickity decision, but one that was in keeping with FIFA's overt instructions about the grab and the grope and the shirt-tug. Behind me an English voice shouted something unintelligible. In front of us Gareth leapt up, then sat down again, remembering himself. A surprisingly gloomy silence fell.

It took three minutes to take the kick. Colombian players converged on the referee, partly out of a sense of injustice, partly out of a desire to stamp down on and mess up the penalty spot, which they did repeatedly as Kane stood to one side holding the ball and remaining remarkably mild in the circumstances. Henderson was booked for complaining. The yellow shirts were waved away, dragged back, cleared from the penalty area. The whole of the Spartak seemed to whistle and jeer as Kane placed the ball carefully, nuzzling the turf around it with his toe. There was a stutter, a quick-stepping run-up and the ball was spanked with bracing power past Ospina.

It was Kane's sixth goal of this World Cup in his third game. The stadium crowd seethed in small red and white pockets. England's players leapt on their captain by the touchline. And like it or not, dismiss his penalties and tap-ins and deflections as all, independently, flukes and one-offs, England did have a star now.

Kane had just become the first England player to score in six successive games since Tommy Lawton in 1939. At that moment he had thirteen goals in his last nine England games, a purple run to match anything any England striker has produced in modern times. Wayne Rooney's best was eleven in ten. George Camsell scored eighteen in nine games in the 1930s and never played again. The peerless Jimmy Greaves got sixteen in eleven at one stage. Gary Lineker went on a jaw-dropping run of seventeen in eleven over eighteen months, bookended by hat-tricks against Poland and Turkey. And now we had Kane, a late-blooming, un-starry, all-round machine of a centre-forward, able to score any type of goal, able to play as a 10 or as a 9. Best of all he'd become a furiously relentless figure, subjecting his marker to the equivalent of a ninety-minute combat session, all turns and bumps and sprints, shots loosed off from the tiniest space, a striker right at the top of his game.

And for a while it looked like this really was heading England's way, albeit not without a little ugliness en route. Five Colombian players had been booked either side of half-time. In slow motion John Stones seemed to have very delicately and accidentally kicked Falcao in the head. Maguire was accused of diving by a posse of Colombian players who seemed shocked, enraged and appalled that such things could happen. The yellow shirts pressed with energy but no precision as the clock ran down, time seeming to slow and sag and forget to move.

With nine minutes left Kyle Walker made a terrible mistake, dawdling on the ball as Bacca pressed. From his pass Cuadrado punted the ball over the bar when he really should have scored. Jamie Vardy came on for Sterling, hoping to take advantage of any breaks as Colombia pushed. But there were no breaks, just a blunt, concussive pressure, and not for the last time a sense that England's substitutions had failed, that Southgate was not best suited to altering the flow of a game. Five minutes of stoppage time were signalled, but it could have been more. At which point two incredible things happened.

First Jordan Pickford produced a save from Mateus Uribe's shot so cinematically good it seems doubly bizarre it was almost immediately erased from the memory. As Uribe shot, Pickford skipped across goal like a ballet dancer, threw up one hand and palmed the ball out for a corner. From the kick Mina leapt above Maguire, propelling himself to somewhere close to seven feet off the ground, then butted the ball down into the ground and up over the head of Trippier on the post. All around us, all across the stands, there was instant delirium. Mina ran to the far side and was almost eaten by the crowd as it surged down towards him. Around me there was silence, the odd groan, the sound of intros being quietly deleted. Half an hour more then. Sweets. We're going to need sweets.

*

Mateus Uribe just needs to score and they're almost there. One more kick to put Colombia 4–2 up, with every penalty after that a bullet for sudden death. Uribe walks from the centre-circle with an unavoidable swagger, product of those bulging thighs. He glances down at the tattoo sleeve on his left arm as he reaches the spot. It has been a meandering journey to this stage for Uribe, a childhood friend of James Rodríguez in Medellín and a late-bloomer as a powerful central midfielder. He plays in Mexico these days, and made his name with a commanding game against France in March when he ran N'Golo Kanté into the ground in the second half. Uribe pauses for a moment, then runs up and smacks the ball hard with the outside of his foot. It's miles out of Pickford's reach, so much so that even in that millisecond he's given it up, letting his hand reach down. But this is also an arrogant kick, hit with an unnecessary, careless power. The ball seems to gain height in the last few feet. It hits the crossbar with a lovely smacking sound and flies away into the Moscow night. Uribe covers his face.

Trippier follows him quickly, marching up in a straight line and spotting the ball. He's not going to miss. Everything about the moment tells you this. And it's a beautiful penalty, struck with the instep high and across Ospina into the top corner. Trippier walks back straight away, a single fist clenched. England are level.

*

As the players gathered in their huddles in front of us Colombia looked happiest to be going to extra-time, and not just because they'd been rescued at the death. Nothing about their game plan had been geared towards the quick kill. José Pékerman, their manager, had always suggested it might be necessary to take this game deep. In the middle of all this it was a treat to see him so close on the touchline, a tall, grey, hawk-like figure, with an arch, austere look about him. Pékerman had made his name as a mentor to some wonderful Argentine players through the youth teams of his homeland. He'd nurtured a little bit of the genius in Lionel Messi. He'd passed on a team that really should have won a World Cup. Oddly enough, standing here in Moscow he was just a few hundred miles from ancestral home soil. The Pékerman grandparents were from Ukraine, part of the immigrant group who would become the nineteenth-century Jewish gauchos of the Entre Ríos province.

Pékerman versus Southgate was fascinating in itself, a first competitive test for England's manager against a coach with the tactical expertise to pull at the seams of his young team. And despite those nine days of rest after Panama for Southgate's first string, it was Colombia who began to creep up through the gears as extra-time ticked on. Vardy was a ghost up front. Eric Dier came in to reinforce the central midfield but seemed unable to imprint himself on any part of the game. Pickford made a good save at Falcao's feet. England were hanging on. Walker went down with cramp. Dier dropped into makeshift defence as Gareth appeared on the touchline at just the right moment, pointing calmly, speaking to Trippier, radiating paternal calm. For a while it was hard to shake the feeling that somehow, whatever the rules might say about it, Southgate was going to run up in his waistcoat and score the winning penalty.

Steadily England pressed back a little, pushing down the left through Danny Rose. Rumours appeared on the internet that Bogotá's El Dorado International Airport had given up and closed down so that everyone could just watch the game. Finally England won a corner, a last chance that saw Dier head wildly over the bar from a decent position. There were shouts of frustration from the seats behind. Two hours into this game everyone was suffering. The final whistle, felt like a weary act of mercy.

Except, something else began to kick in. England's players didn't lie down flat on the ground or look shattered or fall about like a rabble. Gareth didn't walk among them with that familiar panicky sense of purpose or start waving a piece of paper around or asking people if they fancied a penalty, summoning the spirits of Bobby Robson, Terry Venables or Sven-Göran Eriksson, the ultimate spiffy-suited busker. Instead the team gathered in a huddle, quite close to us now, shoulders bowed, orderly and composed. Southgate spoke briefly. The players applauded. Then the red shirts walked briskly to the centre-circle and took up their positions, arm in arm. The endgame was here.

*

The scores are level. Both teams have one kick left. It's now five minutes to midnight. This game really has reached its outer limits. The scenes of people back in England leaping, holding their heads, throwing drinks, huddling in stricken packs, would be replayed through the days to come. In the stadium there's a slight daze in between the yells and screams for each kick, a wash of stale adrenaline from two and a half hours of this gorgeously more-ish intensity. The newspaper desk needs our copy in two minutes. Frankly, by now I really don't care who wins. Just make it quick.

Carlos Bacca is up next for Colombia. Bacca is an experienced player. He's also an evangelical Christian, rumoured to have tried to move to Roma to be nearer the Pope. He's a lovely finisher, a powerful, classical centre-forward. But Bacca has scored only one goal for Colombia, in a friendly against China, in the last two years. He pauses, looks up, steps forward and hits the ball hard and flat and central as Pickford dives away to his right. There's a micro-second as Pickford falls, the ball zinging towards the empty net, where it seems to be in, where Bacca will have seen in his mind the ball entering the net. At which point Pickford does something astonishing, something that exists only in the tiniest fraction of a moment, in the flicker of nerves and the twitch of muscles. As he falls Pickford sees the ball is missing him and raises his left arm, just enough in the no-time he has, and with enough strength to reach up behind the ball, deflecting it up and away as he falls out of reach.

It's the first save by an England goalkeeper in a penalty shoot-out since David Seaman stopped one from Hernán Crespo in the defeat to Argentina in Saint-Étienne in 1998. It is also a stunning reaction. Without that flex of the arm the ball hits the net or, best case, hits Pickford and bounces in, leaving him head in hands at another almost-but-not-quite. It is the kind of fine margin Pickford has trained for. He has suffered his knock-backs, has gone on loan to Alfreton Town and Darlington and struggled against those who said he's too short or too jittery. I saw Pickford make his professional debut for Sunderland against Arsenal in the FA Cup and you could see right away he was unusually athletic, rolling and twirling about like a tumbler. At one point he somehow diverted a shot from Olivier Giroud up over the bar off his stomach. David Moyes told Pickford to stop eating junk and he did. He's still a little raw. But he has natural strength to make up for his lack of extreme height, executing his saves with snap and spring like a martial artist running through his combination-punch routines. Whatever happens from here, he will always have Moscow.

Eric Dier steps up to take England's fifth penalty. There isn't time to take in how unexpected this is. Dier scored from a free-kick at the last Euros, an event that seemed extraordinary then too. He has struggled to push on. He struggled in this game. At times he doesn't look as much a natural-born footballer as a general-purpose athlete. He has a kick now to put England into the quarter-finals of the World Cup. Dier stands side on to the ball, head lowered, like a man contemplating the meaning of oligarchical capitalism in a semi-mixed, top-down economy. The referee chooses this of all moments to become concerned about something over on the far side, scampering across distractingly. Dier bows his head again and hits his penalty just hard enough, just wide enough, a pretty horrible kick in truth but one that still scuds low past Ospina's right hand. And England really have won. They really are still in the World Cup. The tournament's least experienced team has won a shoot-out, and a hard shoot-out too, where your opponent is gnarled and seasoned and keeps on refusing to die.

This felt like a Gareth moment. In many ways it was a triumph of study and method. Southgate educated himself, soaked up the ways and structures of those who know how to win in elite sport. He managed the details, the weather, the variables around the team as much as the tactical tides of the match itself. British sport is good at this. The Olympic programme has sloshed funds on the more rarified technical sports, has invested selectively, glossed its elite talent, opening up to sports science, psychology and every kind of helpful gimmickry. It was temping, as it is now, to point to all this stuff, to talk about systems.

But really, penalties at the Spartak was a triumph of personality, spirit and good sense. At the end Gareth could be seen at the edge of the pitch with his wife, his daughter and son, taking in this rarest of moments. England had won a shoot-out and there wasn't much to say any more about curses and hoodoos, or any need to drill down into the science and semi-science. Best to leave it to Gareth, who chose this moment to speak some pure gold into the cameras, a man completely there in the moment, thinking with a rare kind of clarity.

For the belief of this group of players, and groups of players to come, it was a really important moment. Not just winning the shoot-out, but having to suffer at the end of the game in a stadium that was five-to-one Colombian fans and felt like an away fixture. To come through all of that; we've spoken to the players about writing their own stories. Tonight they showed they don't have to conform to what's gone before. They have created their own history.

10

Brazil and Being the Bad Guys

6 July 2018

There's a famous sketch from the old Mitchell and Webb comedy series where David Mitchell and Robert Webb appear dressed as Waffen-SS soldiers on the Russian front during the Second World War. All is in order. The division seem confident as the Russian advance is about to be crushed. Except one of them is having some doubts. Looking at their gleaming field-grey uniforms, their insignia ('Have you noticed, our caps have actually got little pictures of skulls on them?'), a thought has begun to nag away. Finally he puts it out there. 'Hans. Are we ... the baddies?'

Every drama needs a villain of course. But their identity can sometimes surprise you, even when it appears to be written in vast glowing capitals to everyone else. One of the most surprising turns at Russia 2018 was the identity of the tournament's arch bad guy and all-round pantomime stooge. On balance Neymar might have hoped for a little more from his second World Cup. He remains the highest-paid twenty-six-year-old commodity in the history of the sport. At this World Cup he nudged up past Romário into third place on Brazil's all-time scoring charts, and is now just twenty goals away from overhauling both Ronaldo and Pelé. His life exists inside a gilded world, a business of being ferried from training complex to sealed seven-star hotel in his own yak-fur-lined helicopter gunship.

Neymar is bigger than his club, bigger, as a corporate-celebrity being, than anything that might arrange itself in his path. He is an outsize star without having really become the very best at what he does just yet. He is a performer with fame and commercial clout and Brazil's continental-scale backing, an entity that demands its own space, its own billing, a suitable stage in which to plant itself.

Two years previously I'd watched in Rio as Brazil went absolutely insane for Neymar's Under-23 team over two weeks en route to winning the Olympic gold medal. This was an event that made absolutely zero ripples anywhere else. But it was received back home as a form of ultimate triumph, a mass yellow-shirted Maracanã Stadium willing Neymar's (scuffed) winning penalty across the line in the final to huge squeals, screams, squawks, gasps and general emotional collapse.

The World Cup also felt like a burden to discharge, not least after the appalling humiliation of four years ago and that 7–1 defeat by Germany in Belo Horizonte. But football remains a cussed kind of thing, uncooperative and iconoclastic. In Russia Brazil and Neymar confirmed their status in the wider world as something else, something surprising to those who remember the twentieth-century powerhouse. That sense of romance has now been thoroughly corroded, leaving a more modern-day presence, a team that seems entitled, fading, overhyped; even at times, it seems, the bad guys.

Tite's young team would reach its moment of crisis in Kazan. Before then there was time, once again, to digest and make sense of England. On the night of the Colombia game Moscow was going through one of its muggy periods, those summer days when the air refuses to move, when you suddenly feel how far inland this city is compared with anywhere on our breezy island. Ravenously hungry on the way back from the Spartak, I'd stumbled across Moscow McDonald's, which turned out to be spiffy and up-market when set beside, say, the drive-through at Bell Green Retail Park in Lewisham. Well-dressed Muscovites ordered cheeseburgers and fries. A massive shiny Mercedes jeep purred to the kerb outside, joining the rows of blacked-out mega-cruisers. I made two discoveries. First, McDonald's Moscow does delicious crunchy chicken wings. Second, you still feel like you've eaten a plutonium-soaked squirrel carcass half an hour later.

It was 3.30 am by the time I got back to the flat on Novy Arbat, the sky already turning light at the edges, the traffic pounding down the six-lane highway eleven floors below.

Still chomping through the post-deadline adrenaline, I couldn't really sleep much. It had been a weird night, the kind of night where you appreciate what a brilliant but odd and lonely job it can be at times.

It still surprises me how calm the *Guardian* sport desk is down the line. The football editors Marcus Christensen and Jon Brodkin have a reassuring kind of fatalism about them on occasions like these. 'OK, so if the game goes to extra-time and penalties we'll need nine hundred words on the final penalty either way whoever wins and the page goes five minutes later. Oh, don't worry, it'll be fine.' I still suspect Jon and Marcus didn't actually go home at all through the entire tournament. Whenever I asked them about this they just sort of laughed quietly and changed the subject. But then, everyone was stretched by this, in the best possible way, beavering manically through the wee hours, subs taking panicked copy fudged together close to midnight with a two-hundred-word intro and the names of the goal-scorers wrong, and turning it into something that flows and makes sense and fills a page the next day. Newspaper are criticised a lot for their alleged shoddiness, laziness and generic, cliché-ridden, morally bankrupt obsolescence. But more often than not it only looks easy because the people doing it are so good.

Over a shivery, brain-mangled breakfast the headlines from home still looked a little improbable. BELIEVE. AT LAST! THE HISTORY BOYS. MIRACLE, DREAMLAND. MIRACLE IN MOSCOW. And of course NEW ICE AGE FEAR AS DIANA RIDDLE POINTS

TO HOUSE PRICE CRASH. Winning a penalty shoot-out was one part of this. Another was Gareth's gamble, the resting of players in the Belgium game and a feeling of the draw opening up. England's dressing room was like *The Raft of the Medusa* after the Colombia game, with players strewn across the benches with injuries, exhaustion and cramp. Now they had four days to recover and prepare for a quarter-final against Sweden in the heat of Samara. No international game is easy. But some are less hard than others. The English summer seemed to turn a little dizzier, a little more wild.

*

Elsewhere the World Cup just kept rolling along into the rapid-fire sudden death of the knockout phase. My next stop was back in Nizhny Novgorod for France versus Uruguay and an epic-looking last-sixteen game that turned out to be something closer to a straightforward suffocation. Before then my own thoughts were elsewhere. The same night Brazil would play Belgium in Kazan, a match I'd been feeling uneasy about since it emerged from the draw. Brazil's entire campaign to date had already brought a familiar string of anguished pre-game emails from my father, Brazil's biggest ex-pat Anglo-Hungarian fan, who was watching in Florida.

Brazil had always been my team, at times more so than England. I did have an excuse for this beyond the beauty and fun of those Brazil teams of the 1980s. My dad lived in Brazil the whole time I was growing up. He had a business in São Paulo, back in the old wild days of hyperinflation and hypercorruption and hyper-flaky governments. He grew to love Brazilian football, as did his naturalised English friends out there, many of whom had married Brazilian women or moved to the country for jobs and stayed. I remember one very drunk middle-aged Cockney helicopter salesman cornering me in a bar when I was a kid and talking at great length about the times he'd seen Pelé play in Rio and São Paulo and Recife. 'He had all the skills. He could do anything with the ball. But he was strong, Barn. He was like a bull. A bull. Like a bull, he was. A bull.'

My dad use to send me Brazil shirts and tracksuits. For a while 'Brazil' was my nickname at school. We went to watch Flamengo and Vasco da Gama and felt that strange kind of fever for the first time, watching players who would never come to Europe, whose skills were on a different level to the old First Division fare back home (although my favourite, Dener, would die in a late-night car crash in Rio a few weeks after I'd seen him score a stunning scissor-kick goal at the Maracanã).

Hard as it might be to believe now, Brazil were also hip in those days. For all their trophy-winning ways they also represented a sporting counter-culture, a note of beauty and imagination beyond the bleakness of the mud-bound game. Perhaps it's simply because we didn't see them much in those days, a group of footballers who only existed every four years, or here and there in UEFA competitions lurking in the ranks of some glamorous Italian superpower. For decades everyone who loved football, who actually *loved* it, who saw it as something uplifting and free, was on the side of Brazil.

'We have nothing to learn from the Brazilians,' Charles Hughes famously announced during his days as FA technical director and high priest of the long-ball creed in English football. This felt like an ideological opposition, freedom versus control, imagination versus dunderheaded discipline, Little Englander-dom versus the riches of the world. If this seems gauche and laughable to anyone under the age of thirty given Brazil's current status as the co-opted, corporate, sponsor-obsessed feeder industry for the European club game – as, in effect, the bad guys – it was probably fairly sketchy then too.

Either way the obsession in Brazil with football and with a sixth World Cup win remained as strong as ever, even at a tournament that had started with a whisper of familiar angst. Brazil's opening game against Switzerland in Rostov was an odd thing. Brazil took the lead through a brilliant goal from Philippe Coutinho. They kept the ball. They started to embroider and even showboat a little. Switzerland were unimpressed. Switzerland kicked Neymar up in the air for a while. Brazil became distracted. Switzerland equalised deservedly in the second half though Steven Zuber. And Brazil travelled to St Petersburg for their second group game against Costa Rica as another of the tournament favourites still to click into gear, mocked a little, jeered at by neutrals. Already there was a disproportionate focus on Neymar, not least on his absurd golden-spaghetti-crown hairstyle, which would be abruptly removed in time for the next game.

How Football (Nearly) Came Home

The St Petersburg Stadium is out on the water at the edge of the Gulf of Finland, lodged beside the endless cantilevered bridge that swoops in above the tide and funnels the main traffic arteries into the city centre. The stadium is a stunning thing, another enormo-dome, with the most astonishing roof fanned out around steel girders of dizzying scale, like a vast iron giant cradling his fingers.

The stands were the usual wallpaper-setting of Brazil gold, broken up by some enthusiastic blocks of Costa Rican red. There was a sudden whirling gust of noise as Brazil kicked off with the pitch half in shadow, half in bright afternoon sun, a classic World Cup trope for those raised on shots of Mexico 70 and Mexico 86, when the analogue TV picture would leap with finger-twiddling haste between dazzling light and sudden patches of refocused gloom.

At which point things began to go sour, slowly at first, but with a gathering momentum. This would turn out to be Neymar's game, and not in a good way, as Brazil's captain produced an extraordinary World Cup performance. Again, not in a good way.

Brazil had made one change, Fagner replacing the injured Danilo at right-back. Roberto Firmino, so little regarded in his own country after a footballing life spent in Europe, remained on the bench. There were some early collisions as Costa Rica tried to assert their physicality. Casemiro took a blow in the face and came back on with tissue paper sticking out of his bloodied nose.

For a while Neymar tried just playing football, running at the left-hand side of Costa Rica's defence. But slowly something else began to intrude. Neymar was writhing and leaping at every challenge, amplifying his response to every contact. With half an hour gone he tricked his way to the edge of the area and simply hurled himself down, burying his face in the turf in apparent agony. There was another horrible dive as he went past Gamboa, who reacted furiously. At half-time the cameras caught Neymar jabbering away at the referee Björn Kuipers outside the dressing room, watched by some apparently helpless Brazil backroom staff, gawping at their celebrity leader when he really should have been hauled into the dressing room and told to stop falling over and get his act together for the team.

And so it went on. Tite took off Willian at half-time and put on the more direct Douglas Costa, changing the game in the process. But still the focus was on Neymar and some frankly ludicrous antics. Every time Neymar got the ball the pattern was the same. A feather-footed touch. Brilliantly easy acceleration, with the balance and grace of a player made entirely from icing sugar and daisy petals, the ball control perfect, head up, options opening, a moment and a game to be seized. At which point, enter cartwheels, high jumps, squeals, gut-wrenching agony, a whirl of finger pointing and berating the referee, all accompanied by constant TV close-ups of that delicately pained face. No wonder people tired of this, saw a footballer intent on seeing his sport as a series of fouls interrupted by brief periods of dribbling.

Around the hour mark referee Kuipers finally snapped. As Costa Rica prepared to take a corner he strode over, wagging his finger, and told Neymar to stop whinging and swearing at opponents, in much the same way you might address a group of noisy teenagers in the back row at the multiplex.

Then something strange happened. Giancarlo González brushed Neymar's stomach with his hand in the penalty area. At which point Brazil's No. 10 simply collapsed, falling backwards like a man shot seventeen times in the chest by a high-calibre automatic rifle. A penalty was awarded as Neymar lay prone on the turf being tended to by his teammates, a precious dying prince, victorious finally in his battle with the higher powers.

Except things were taking an odd turn. Kuipers returned to the pitch from a quick look at his VAR screen and changed his mind. No penalty. As was only correct. Brazil's players and fans and management were aghast, but really they should be better than this, should be better than addressing a football match as though it is a matter of accumulating fouls and browbeating the officials.

In stoppage time, as Costa Rica tired, Brazil scored twice. First Coutinho spanked a loose ball past Keylor Navas from close range, sparking a vast bundle and an inadvertent celebration somersault by the manager Tite on the touchline. And with seven minutes of overtime played Neymar tapped into an open goal, then collapsed in a weeping huddle on the grass, shoulders shaking, hands hiding his face, gripped with a huge and impressively potent cheesy smorgasbord of overblown emotion. It was in that moment, as the world hurled its half-eaten sandwich at the

TV screen, that Neymar was crystallised as the bad guy, as something un-manly and un-football, an acme of preening and entitled superstardom.

This is a big part of Brazil's journey from popular heroes and cartoon good guys. To put it bluntly, they have become a bunch of wet lettuces. The most stirring part of Brazil's home World Cup four years ago was the surrounding noise, the atmosphere of relentless hysteria, a World Cup drenched in hot wet salty tears. Goals were greeted by prayers and emotional collapses. Operatic anxiety swirled around the stands from the first game at the cavernous, still-unfinished Arena de São Paulo. In part this was the fearful burden of history and expectation. In part it felt like vanity, Brazil's desire to place itself at the centre of things, football's great Viking-horned, chest-heaving diva. In 2014 it was clear Brazil were almost done before the Colombia game when Thiago Silva burst into tears at the pre-match press conference.

Four years on, the team's emotional state was still an object of constant frowning debate. At Tite's press conference before the Costa Rica game the opening question had been about exactly what degree of crying should be permitted among the players, what were the official Brazilian FA weeping guidelines. Thiago Silva himself had been vocal in his support of the right to weep. 'Tite cried after the first match,' Tite had admitted, talking about Tite in the third person. But then being involved with Brazil in any form at a World Cup, right down to being jostled by the massed ranks of the Globo Esporte media team in the queue for a vending-machine packet of salted-potato-chip products, is to find yourself sucked into this drama of joy, collapse and emotional exhaustion.

Even the press conferences are a test of stamina, the questions impossibly long and nuanced ('And my second part of this question is, do you, Professor, believe that...'). Everyone calls Tite 'professor'. He's not actually a professor, but he does like examining every possible angle of every possible implied scenario in an endless degree of detail. Part of this is a simple mania for his sport. By domestic managerial standards Tite is a real moderniser. He travelled the European club game, visiting the top managers, learning at the feet of Pep Guardiola, absorbing the science. Somehow though, his Brazil also seemed receptive to the worst of elite club football. At times Brazil 2018 presented a gruesome funfair-mirror version of the club football star system, most notably in the absurd degree of indulgence and veneration extended towards Neymar.

More to the point, it just isn't supposed to be this way. Brazil are not this – or weren't this. As social media crowed and sneered at these damp-eye princelings, as columnists and commentators poured scorn on Brazil's fragility and arrogance, it felt like a double betrayal. Brazil are supposed to be more emotionally honest, an expression of something more uplifting. They're supposed to be the good guys. The first time they played England was in a friendly at Wembley in May 1956, during which Brazil's Álvaro was so upset by the award of a penalty he grabbed hold of the ball and refused to give it back, only relenting after his team-mates

Brazil and Being the Bad Guys

'talked him down' over several long minutes. An England team containing Stanley Matthews and Duncan Edwards won the game 4–2. 'Another victory for teamwork against brilliant individuals,' the Pathé newsreel footage of the day concluded, a little disdainfully.

But two years later Brazil would win their first World Cup in Sweden, driven on by the seventeen-year-old Pelé. And down the years Brazil teams were not cry-babies and milksops and princelings. They were tough and seasoned and clever and resilient. The great 1982 team of Sócrates and Éder and Falcão was full of grizzled, tiny-shorted, charismatic men. Brazilians generally, in my experience, are not these precious, highly strung adolescents. We remember Leônidas, the Black Diamond of the 1930s, who drew crowds of young women to Brazil's matches, many of them, if the stories were true, likely to be fond personal acquaintances. Garrincha had as much fun as anyone on a football pitch, as did Rómario in the hours he was off it. These were tough, roguish players. Watching Rivellino swagger about the pitch with such rakish malevolence you half expected to look down and notice he was still in his dressing-gown, baseball bat in one hand, bottle of bourbon in the other.

And so on to Neymar. He wasn't meant to be like this. The most remarkable thing about him at that 2014 World Cup, when he was twenty-two and had the world on his shoulders, was his ability to let this pressure slide off him, to remain opaque, cheerful and fully revved. Watching him in Salvador and São Paulo I remember David Hytner and me really getting him for the first time, falling in love with his movement and his ballsiness and basic joy in all this. At times the idea of calling footballers 'players' can strike you as quite funny. There is very little that is playful in modern football, very little that is improvised or spontaneous. These people are not playing. They are minutely instructed employees, high-level physical workers, units for kicking and running. But Neymar *was* playing at that World Cup. He'd take the ball in his stride with his instep and back-spin it out in front of him just for fun, in the middle of a game where everyone else seemed to be stricken with eye-bulging terror.

It is worth remembering, as ever, that so much of the story in football is reverse-engineered out of details. Neymar went to the 2018 World Cup unfit and was clearly rusty when he got there, frustrated by his lack of match edge. In his best form we might have seen a more joyful, robust, inspiring footballer. The previous November he had played against England at Wembley and looked at his most carefree. At one point he tracked back to the corner flag, took the ball off Marcus Rashford, danced past Kyle Walker with a lovely little half-step and ran the ball sixty yards upfield without even seeming to breathe.

There were glimpses of this in the final group game in Moscow against Serbia. Brazil at least played like a team. They were solid in the clinches against opponents field-ing a central midfield with the combined height of three small men in Nemanja Matić and Sergej Malinković-Savić. Coutinho set up Paulhino for the opening goal. Thiago Silva headed the second. Neymar ran hard and kept his counsel.

Brazil and Being the Bad Guys

He played better in Samara in the first knockout round against Mexico, the day before England played Colombia. Mexico have often troubled Brazil and this was a team packed with pace and fight. The game was goalless at half-time. At which point Neymar did the best thing he did all World Cup, picking the ball up on the left, skipping inside, beating his man, shaping to shoot, but instead back-heeling the ball – a good back-heel, a non-gratuitous back-heel – to Willian in space. His cross found Neymar, who scored. This looked like Brazil, the good Brazil, a team of technicians whose best qualities are mischievous and creative. Roberto Firmino got the second in a 2–0 win from Neymar's scuffed shot-cum-assist.

And everything might have been on track and back in gear. Except, once again there was the enraging spectacle of Neymar writhing about on his back like a dying wood-louse, playing right at the edge of the rules of the game and basically driving everyone to distraction. This time it was a ludicrous altercation with Miguel Layún, a second-half substitute who stepped on the prone – he was already writh-ing around – Neymar's ankle as he picked up the ball by the touchline. Neymar reacted like a man injected with ten thousand volts, possessed by ghouls, speaking in tongues, rolling around with genuinely impressive vim and energy in an attempt to get Layún sent off. In the event he probably saved Layún from a red card, so irritating were his antics.

And so back to where we came in, to Nizhny Novgorod and the night before England in Samara. Uruguay versus France passed in a blur. Didier Deschamps sent his team out to win while expending the least energy. A goal either side of half-time from Raphaël Varane and Antoine Griezmann was enough. Back in the media centre in a city we would leave in three hours' time, having flown in that morning, Stuart James and I had one of those moments of existential tournament doubt. Did anyone care that we were out here doing this stuff? Why were we here? What were we here? How were we here? And how were we going to get to the airport in time?

Before then, though, it was time to clear space by one of the FIFA TVs, put my feet up on a small plastic stool and watch Brazil and Belgium in Kazan. This was a powerful Belgium team in every sense. The midfield was stiffened by the presence of Marouane Fellaini, the footballing equivalent of the pair of dirty wellies you keep in the boot of the car for days like these. With Brazil's own muscular pivot Casemiro out suspended, it worked too. Fellaini, Axel Witsel and Nacer Chadli just ran over Brazil in the opening half-hour of a grippingly open game. Fernandinho's slightly bizarre own goal gave Belgium the lead in the thirteenth minute, the ball headed into Brazil's net under no pressure at a corner.

Neymar zigzagged down the left and almost set up Jesus for an equaliser. Eden Hazard tortured Brazil's left side, showing that astonishing ability to spring sideways, hurdle challenges, bump off his markers, a player who seemed closer to the ground than anyone else on the pitch, running on legs fashioned from superior muscles and tendons.

With half an hour gone De Bruyne made it 2–0 with a

laughably brilliant fizzed shot into the bottom-left corner, a goal made by Lukaku's movement and power. Brazil were being pummelled, outrun, out-moved and made to look the callow, weepy team of their lowest moments. This felt like a thoroughly modern machine revving its way past something more brittle and patched together, Europe versus the best of the rest.

To his credit Neymar threw himself into the retreat from Kazan. The yellow shirts poured forward and got one back through Renato Augusto's header. With ninety-four minutes on the clock, Neymar had his moment that might have been. Douglas Costa rolled the ball across the face of the area. Neymar adjusted the lean of his body and curled the ball with his left foot towards the top corner, only for Thibaut Courtois to palm it over the bar.

And that was that for another strange, fractious, oddly overwrought Brazilian World Cup. Brazil are still an event, a part of the World Cup finery to be fanfared in and out. But in Russia they felt like something for the first time. This was a team that gave the greatest pleasure to the most people by exiting the tournament, victims of their own star culture, of some unappealing on-field habits, a feeling that these are now decisively one of football's overdogs.

As for Neymar, the next-best, next-best player in the world, the tournament was a statistical oddity. He was fouled more times per minute than any other player by some distance, although this does stretch the definition of being fouled to its furthest extreme. Somehow he also had the most shots on goal, with twenty-seven to Harry

Kane's sixteen and Kylian Mbappé's eight. To put this in context, Mbappé played two more games and scored twice as many goals.

But then, in a way Deschamps' France were a kind of rebuttal of the individualism of club football culture. Although not so much in the day job, where Neymar had spent the season as the star turn in a team obsessed with star power in a French league skewed by the marketing ambitions of an energy super-state. I'd been in Paris six months before the World Cup to watch Neymar play for PSG against poor old Dijon, a team with a £450 million attack against one that had never spent more than £2 million on a player.

There were playful boos towards the end as Neymar stepped up to take a penalty. PSG were 7–0 up at the time and Neymar already had a hat-trick, including a delicious winding run and finish past five players from the halfway line, the high point of a year spent simply being Neymar, football's most peculiarly frictionless megastar.

As we scattered for the airport, Nizhny Novgorod had already begun to pack up. Its World Cup was done, the volunteers in the media centre already larking about, taking selfies, emptying their lockers. The desks would be gone the next day, the fittings packed away. There were six teams left in the World Cup and nine days still to play. Now it was England's turn again.

11

O Happy Day

7 July 2018

Sometimes the sun also rises. The Colombia game had been startling and unforgettable. It still feels like the heart, the meat, the rump, the spine, the vital organs of England's World Cup. It also felt strangely more-ish. Even thinking about that night at the Spartak three months on brings on a tremor. There's an urge to reach for the YouTube tab, to dig out another jerkily shot crowd-film of that penalty shoot-out, tee it up, pump up the volume and suck it down into the lungs like a dose of cool white smoke.

At the same time it was also pretty gruelling to watch, let alone play in, a night that left you walking around with a cramp in your brain for the next two days. The group games had been fun and light and easy on the ears. Colombia was this England team's difficult third album, something more painful and tortured, from its extended build-up to those crazed last knockings close to midnight.

Five days later we moved on to the distant south-west and another stage in this unexpected journey. Samara was an awkward place to get to. Direct flights were scarce. Trains were overbooked. From Moscow it was an eight-hundred-mile trip in the general direction of the Kazakhstan border. My return ticket took me there via somewhere called Mineralnye Vody, a semi-rural spa town on the road to Azerbaijan, which is also, coincidentally, the title of one of the lesser-known Bing Crosby and Bob Hope movies.

Samara had been another of Soviet Russia's closed cities, a place where the military developed its missile shield against nuclear attack. These days it is a dusty, prosperous city with a famous waterfront and a run-down periphery with rows of antique jerry-built houses. For the England fans, staying wherever they could find a room, kipping on floors and paying through the nose for what hotel rooms remained, it turned out to be a lovely place to camp out in the downtown bars; and to watch a World Cup quarter-final against Sweden that felt like something else entirely after the tension of Colombia.

This was the other thing about Samara – a different kind of noise, something just out of earshot beneath the clamour. High up in the stands of the Cosmos Arena before kick-off you could see blue all around, the sky fading to white at the edges, and the start of the green fringes of town off to the east where the Volga bends around. The sun had begun to sink but the air was still heavy with the kind of heat that makes you feel a little drunk and full and sleepy just breathing it in.

The Cosmos is a brand new spacey-looking thing dumped down in a flat concrete field. In an odd twist it seemed to have been built as an exact replica of the Millennium Dome in Greenwich, which you can see from my front garden at home – but an evil replica, the Millennium Dome that turns into a giant alien egg and tries to destroy Washington DC. I drank a very cold bottle of Sprite in the top of the stand, while down below the first group of England fans staked out their corner, basking in the sun, strolling the concourses. And that background noise was still there, the sense of something else just starting to clarify.

Back home the Colombia game seemed to have broken the seal. Diego Maradona had described England's victory as 'a monumental theft'. He later apologised, saying he was 'overwhelmed' at the time, which is certainly one way of putting it. Otherwise it was all going off now. That caution, the fear of the jinx, the furrowed reticence. Well, that was history. My *Guardian* colleague Hadley Freeman wrote that an American friend had watched the reaction to the Colombia victory and compared England to 'one of those crazy people who goes on a good date and immediately starts planning the wedding'.

And it's true, perhaps this was a little overblown: the triumphalism, the singing in the streets, the endless discussion of the exact, the precise meaning of reaching the last eight of the World Cup by beating Panama and Tunisia. But then, these were not rational times. The high-summer weather refused to break. People came out into the streets and parks and pubs. In London Shoreditch High Street was closed by an impromptu mass rendition of 'Three Lions', which was, of course, everywhere, although suddenly people were also singing the Southgate song, to the tune of Atomic Kitten's 'Whole Again', the song the fans had been singing behind the goal when Gareth came out after the Colombia game to wave and bow and grin before running back to talk to the press.

> *Looking back on when we first met,*
> *I cannot escape and I cannot forget,*
> *Southgate, you're the one,*
> *You still turn me on,*
> *And football's coming home again.*

OK, it's not exactly 'Jerusalem'. But it's probably, on balance, better than the original. And this was Gareth's time, peak Gareth, the acme of Gareth. The image of England's manager consoling Mateus Uribe on the touchline after his missed penalty had been seized on, gushed over and fanfared as an icon of sportsmanship and fraternal manliness, a little hysterically in truth. This kind of thing happens quite a lot. People are constantly hugging and patting each other in sport. But then, we wanted to believe.

By now Gareth was radiating his own kind of light, a coach in that perfect moment of sweetness, where events seem to arrange themselves around him, where every decision seems to drip with deeper meaning. Southgate's triumph was to manage the details of his team to perfection, to select ruthlessly, with an eye on character and resourcefulness, and to create an actual team culture, the rarest of things in a national team so often riven with egotism and brittle methods. Southgate had always carried himself well, been generous and spoken with clarity and good sense. Believe it or not, lots of people are like this in sport. This is a place where character is tested, where virtues are often rewarded and where there is quite a lot to be learnt from those who succeed in the right way. It's just that everyone was listening now.

For those of us covering this the contrast was stark. To be England manager has so often been to experience a kind of public breakdown, a shared neurosis of blame and rejection. England managers never really deserve what they get. But they get it all the same, good or bad. On the eve of this World Cup Gabriel Clarke's excellent documentary about Bobby Robson had captured the disarray at the start of Italia 90. The last time England reached the last four of a World Cup Robson was simultaneously pilloried in the press for lining up a post-England job and humiliated over tales of an extra-marital affair. That tournament kicked off with a furious FA press conference presided over by the chief executive Graham Kelly, a man who resembled not so much an elite sports administrator as a particularly sullen giant hamster forced into a blazer and a fat nylon tie and charged with the job of making English football look as comically detached from reality as possible.

This time around the love was tangible, even a little

schmaltzy. People wrote articles about Gareth and modern manhood. 'The England manager's old-school politeness and modern emotional intelligence are just what a divided nation needs,' an op-ed in *The Times* stated, in all seriousness. Southgate's England were, we were told, a perfect reflection of the best, most instructive sense of Englishness. People who voted remain said he embodied the best of Remain. Marks & Spencer sold out of waistcoats in their branches. Somebody started a petition for a statue and (of course) a knighthood. And naturally there was an urge to see in all this some wider meaning, the moral dimension, the idea that England had won matches because their spirit is righteous, their hearts full, their methods pure, that this team meant things about Brexit and the ability of modern man to express his feelings and so on. Things that presumably they wouldn't have meant if Tunisia had defended better at corners, or Colombia hit a couple of penalties slightly better.

If this sounds churlish or out of kilter with the national mood, it has to be said that none of it was immediately translatable in Russia. We saw the delirium back home second-hand, in web clips and headlines. But in the flesh there was an element of double-take. England's players were a personable bunch. They were better organised. They beat teams they were supposed to beat. They were likeable and fun. Watching them close up you appreciated the focus and the precision. But it still felt a little strange marrying all of that to all of this; looking back from the wildest enthusiasms to the reality of a nice, hard-working bunch of blokes playing at their level and very obviously enjoying themselves.

Again you got the feeling this was about release, escapism, people sucking the sweetness out of the moment at a time when so many other moments have been so much more dour and difficult. For the first time now there was even a vague sense of misgiving about what might happen if this kept on going, how people would react to even more. Sitting up late in Moscow two days after Colombia, the thought suddenly occurred. What would actually happen, how would we cope, how far would it all go if England did reach the final?

In Samara that tension seemed to have passed. Looking down as the crowd began to thicken and the subs and coaches and third goalies came out to cheers and a rustle of applause, there was that sense again of something else underneath it all, a change of pitch.

In the last twenty-four hours I'd come via Moscow, Nizhny Novgorod, then back to Moscow, with three hours' sleep at the airport, then up again a little dizzy and parched for another battle through the departure gates. It's a winding ninety-minute cab journey into the city from Samara airport. My rented room was in a tower block in the centre of what I can only describe as a kind of genteel Soviet favela. But it was clean and jolly, and decorated with framed 1950s nudes, which was a nice homely touch.

Olga, my host, told me not to linger by the stairs late at night and not to use the lift if I could avoid it. I walked five blocks and found the FIFA hotel, with its smart doorman and its bar serving floury chips and gritty calamari to England fans. I was starting to feel a bit floaty as I got the FIFA shuttle from the hotel to the stadium. Emerging into the heat of the carpark I waltzed through security thinking, yes yes, this is all going fine, it's going to be good. At which point, with a sudden sense of total collapse, I realised I'd lost my laptop bag. Twenty-seven days and two and a half thousand miles to get there. And I'd turned up without a computer.

Brain whirling, I ran back to see if it was on the bus, but the bus had parked in a row with twenty other identical ones, most with their curtains drawn and their drivers getting down to the serious business of sleeping for the next four hours. I banged on the doors of the nearest one and woke up a large, bearded man in a vest and a driver's cap. Once he'd understood what I was raving about he started bustling about waking up the others. Together, with a posse of sleepy, puzzled Russian bus drivers, we began working our way through the fleet, searching the seats, issuing urgent, barked Russian commands.

At which point I remembered something. In the blur of the morning I'd left the laptop bag at the favela. The rucksack on my back was quite heavy. A quick peek inside. Yes, there it was. Not actually lost at all, just in a different bag. These are two different, but very important things. I looked at the drivers earnestly searching their buses and shooing their colleagues out, with a terrible, helpless gratitude. At which point, squaring my shoulders, I took the coward's option. Bowing furiously, making apologetic gestures, I basically ran off, leaving them to scratch their heads and go back to sleep. And yes. I'm not proud.

The teams had dropped by now. Dele Alli was back after his thigh injury. Sweden had Celtic right-back Mikael Lustig suspended, his place taken by Emil Krafth. Also absent, it was clear by now, were at least 10,000 paying spectators. There were some good reasons for this. Russia were playing just after this game. England's fans still hadn't travelled in large numbers, partly because of fear, partly because Samara was so hard to get to. Many were stranded in arrival lounges around Europe, last-minute dashes thwarted by airline snags and missed connections.

As the players stood for the anthems, cooled by the evening wind, there was something quite fun and intimate about the sound coming from both sides. In the absence of a few thousand neutrals Sweden's yellow block had filled out the end to our right and England's fans had decked their end with the usual patchwork of flags and banners. The England players were under orders here to sing the national anthem as loudly as they could, to shake the rafters, or at the very least move their mouths with the proper enthusiasm, like pub-curious dads at the Christmas Eve carol service. As they sang you felt for the first time the intimacy of the occasion. Even out here in this brand-new bowl miles outside town at the back end of the Volga, it felt a bit like a private party.

Sweden coach Janne Andersson had been dubbed 'The Monster' for his discipline and his touchline manner. In the opening moments he stood up below us and hollered furiously across at his defence and you felt the force of his urgency. For a while nothing much happened, the ball ferried about in pedestrian fashion, the players getting the feel of the ground and the day. Sweden's front trio pressed Jordan Pickford as he took the ball at his feet, but fell back as he cleared it quite comfortably. This isn't the way to go with Pickford. I saw him ping those flat, hard fifty-yard passes when he first came through at Sunderland, so accurate with the ball at his feet you started to wonder if perhaps he might be better off in a rugby shirt, floating the ball into the corners, easing it between the posts.

Jordan Henderson earned himself a ticking-off from the referee Björn Kuipers for moaning over minor details. Sweden had spoken at their training camp before this game of trying to 'target' and 'neutralise' Harry Kane, identified by the keen-eyed Swedish intelligence machine as an England goal threat. No shit, Svenlock. Before Samara Kane had scored with all six of his shots on target, in the process tracking up 70 per cent of England's tournament goals. But he'd also been traumatised a little by the Colombia game, spending the last half hour running around basically on one leg.

England were solid rather than fluid in the opening period. This was a tough, athletic, well-drilled Sweden – or to put it another way this was Sweden, a team that tends to win when the game goes deep, when they take you to places you don't want to go, the red zone where plans and tactics start to fall apart, anxiety and lactic acid taking over.

England needed to force the day their way, and it was

Raheem Sterling who started the shift of gear, picking up the ball around halfway and running at Sweden's defenders, tactfully skirting Andreas Granqvist. Kane dragged a shot wide. England pressed a little more. 'We're going to Moscow,' the England end sang, as they'd been saying for some time, and indeed as they already had for the Colombia game.

Gradually that background hum began to assert itself, to become a little clearer on a day where you could feel the gravity heading only one way. For England's players and fans it was just one of those sunlit days, a day without edges. This was the change of pitch, the noise underneath it all. And before long you started to realise what it was, that noise. This was England's happy game.

It is a rare thing, and not always obvious at first. The natural state of the football fan is discontent, fatalism, gloom, misery and brooding paranoia. Nobody comes to this sport looking for blue skies and seamless good-news stories. But sometimes you do still get them, those days where it all just flows, where every detail feels soft. For one day in high summer, down in the distant south-west of Russia, it was England's time to drown in honey.

The opening goal came without much warning, but somehow you always felt it coming. Kieran Trippier forced a corner on the right. Ashley Young took the kick, punting it in hard and flat in the new England style, a corner to attack and to try to score from, not a vague lump into the box. England had formed what Glenn Hoddle would refer to, with impeccable vinyl-era-music-lover credentials, as their 'Love Train'. Half of England's outfield players stood in a line near the penalty spot while the yellow shirts jostled and blocked and tried to disrupt the carriages.

While the others rushed off Harry Maguire just waited and found the space opening up in front of him. The ball was placed perfectly. There was a glorious downward thunk of a header, right out of the meat of his forehead. Jamie Vardy would spend much of the tournament referring to Maguire, affectionately, as 'Slabhead'. And as Maguire made contact the interaction of ball and forehead seemed to generate its own hugely satisfying noise, a deep, booming thunk, like the sound of a frozen cow carcass being hurled from a seventeenth-floor window onto a set of cobbles.

The net billowed cinematically. For a moment everyone just seemed to stand and watch it. And then England's players were off, running towards the corner flag. In the press seats people laughed in disbelief at another set-piece goal, shrugged at the brilliance of the header and the feeling of a day that was starting to head one way.

It felt fitting that Maguire should score in Samara. When people at home said they liked this team, that the sullenness of previous generations had been erased and replaced with something more charming, Maguire seemed to embody this. He is an unusually likeable, well-balanced kind of bloke. A little adversity never hurts in this regard. Maguire was not a prodigy, was never the subject of any real kind of fanfare. At school he was an A* student. His teachers thought he might become an accountant, but never really a footballer. He had his breakthrough season in the

Championship, and was heading back there with a relegated Hull City twelve months before England went to Russia. Best of all he just has something oddly endearing about him. Britain had no political presence at the World Cup as part of the boycott following the poisoning in Salisbury. Lindsay Skoll, Britain's forty-seven-year-old deputy ambassador to Russia, was the most senior diplomat present, and she quickly became besotted with Maguire after meeting him at England's training base. 'There is something about him,' Mrs Skoll enthused. 'There's something a bit boyish. He was absolutely charming.'

With England 1–0 up, the game meandered towards half-time. The Swedes looked fretful and frazzled, unable to keep the ball, a team feeling the moment disappear right in front of them. England barely extended themselves, recycling the ball through that pocket in the centre of the three-man defence, saving their sweat. For a while Trippier romped unchecked down the right. Sterling continued to run hard, disorientating a concrete-booted Swedish defence.

And England were happy at half-time, 1–0 up against a Sweden team you always expect to beat like this, by a narrow margin in a scrappy game, a header from a corner, a series of wholehearted collisions. That's how Sweden die. This is their destiny. Around us it felt like everyone was just enjoying the day. The stadium was like a warm bath, the sun dipping a little, the sky a deeper blue. People laughed at pictures of the Gareth Southgate impersonator in the crowd, which had emerged on social media.

The Gareth doppelgänger had been spotted in the bars of Samara the night before, drinking with fans and strolling the pavements.

It really was a striking resemblance, from the hair to the waistcoat and wedding suit to the general courtly demeanour. It emerged later he was an airline pilot from Surrey called Neil Rowe who had been mistaken for Southgate for years, right back to Euro 96, when he ended up signing autographs on napkins just to make people go away. In Russia, as Gareth's stock soared, he embraced the look to an uncanny degree. Although not everyone was in on it. One English journalist came back from nipping down the stadium toilets at half-time looking pale and preoccupied. 'You won't guess,' he said eventually, 'who I was just stood next to at the urinals.'

And so the day rolled on. Pickford saved brilliantly at the start of the second half, clawing away Marcus Berg's header from the foot of his post. With the wing-backs playing high up the pitch England's width kept dragging Sweden's covering midfielders across, leaving holes for the inside-forwards. For six or seven minutes everything just seemed to work, the machine beginning to purr. England forced a succession of corners, kept the ball, switched the game from side to side. You could feel it coming. Suddenly they were all over Sweden, driving them dizzy, forcing panicked clearances.

The Swedish players were getting puffed and dizzy. 'They're going to score again,' someone said and it was riveting in those few moments, a passage of play that would turn out to be England's most fluent of the whole World Cup.

The second goal duly arrived on fifty-eight minutes, headed in this time by Alli. It was the climax to a beautifully worked series of switches from wing to wing, waiting for the slip, the moment of space as Sweden buckled. Jesse Lingard took Trippier's cut-back and crossed instantly. The ball was flighted to the back post, dipping to the edge of the six-yard box. Alli had slipped the cover and buried it with a flex of the neck muscles.

It was a lovely moment for Alli. Against Colombia he'd worked hard without finding any real freedom. This was his best moment for England to date, a first really telling glimpse of a high-grade talent that has felt a little underexplored in the national team. Perhaps understandably. The trauma of Iceland two years ago had been Alli's seventh start, his third in a competitive game. Before this tournament he'd only played a full ninety minutes for England nine times, and done so already under three different managers.

After the goal he ran across to the England fans and did a *Fortnite* dance, something that will take a great deal of careful explanation to future generations studying the grainy 2D highlights. Someone put 'Football's Coming Home' on over the PA. I decided to write an intro linking this spacey, floaty feeling of an England semi-final place to Russia's own space programme – the sense of being propelled above the earth, of looking down on all this gorgeous blue, of being over the moon – in a carefully balanced, semi-ironical nod to lunar flight and 1970s football. It all worked quite well until someone emailed me once it was published to point out that the moon programme was actually based in Kazan, three hundred miles away. But these are details.

Everyone was cooked by now. On the far side the England crowd was rolling around the stands in a hugging, bouncing group, like a happy, sunburnt caterpillar. Down below us Gareth paced his rectangle, frowning and stroking his chin, as ever strangely touching in his shiny blue three-piece. Pickford produced another brilliant save, this time from Viktor Claesson's shot. Fabian Delph came on, days after flying back to be with the squad after his wife had given birth to their third child. 'She's a machine,' Delph would later explain in his post-match interview.

Slowly the minutes ambled down. Below us the red shirts moved in their easy patterns. John Guidetti came on for Sweden, played for half an hour and completed two passes. Sterling ran some more, then came off to warm applause. As World Cup quarter-finals go this had turned into a lazy, drowsy summer Sunday on the chaise longue with the curtains flapping and a crackly jazz record on the gramophone.

The final whistle came in a languid peep, as the players crumpled to their knees on the turf. Sweden had been poor. This was a team that had forgotten its best qualities at just the wrong moment, in much the same way as England at so many tournaments from Shizuoka to Charleroi to Nice.

But not this time. We stood and watched for a bit on the steps, peering out over the rim of the stadium roof, then looking down to watch as the players waved at the crowd. One or two stepped over the railings into the seats to hug their families. Kyle Walker did some funny dancing. The England fans stayed and cheered.

It felt good just to let the moment sink in, the kind of sporting memory that stays down the years, becoming a part of the shared folksy history of English football. This Southgate team really was in a World Cup semi-final, twenty-eight years on from the last one. For Gareth in particular it was a career-defining, life-marking, future-shaping moment. This would always be his whatever happened from here. It was a bookend to Wembley and Euro 96 and Terry Venables holding his shoulders and trying to console him as Germany's players bounced around in the background. Afterwards, leaning back behind his press conference plinth, a little spent for the first time, he kept talking about those who had gone before, his respect for Bobby Robson, his affection for Terry Venables, his sympathy for Roy Hodgson.

By the time I got back to the favela fireworks were popping down the street and Russia and Croatia were heading into a penalty shoot-out in Sochi. Earlier Denis Cheryshev had scored one of the goals of the World Cup to send the Russian volunteers in the Samara media centre into table-banging fits of joy. Extra-time ended with the score 2–2, Mário Fernandes having headed a very late equaliser for the hosts. The bar at the bottom of my building was packed out onto the street with people standing in the darkness watching the endgame on the screens inside.

They cheered Russia's successful penalties. They sat grimly through Croatia pulling level then edging in front. As Ivan Rakitić put away the winning kick there was an extraordinary response. The Russians in the bar didn't weep or hold their heads. They didn't make a sound. They just walked off immediately in silence as though nothing was happening. Even the commentator didn't say anything. Within seconds the street was empty. Ancient Russian stoicism: available now in World Cup penalty-shoot-out form.

The next morning I flagged down a taxi and washed up at the airport in time to fight through the various queues. Russian airports are like a version of Blake and his doors of perception. Behind the doors are other doors. And beyond these are further doors. And beyond those doors, through some others, is the one you actually need to get to with the only working machine that can print your boarding pass.

The final departure lounge at Samara airport is a huge, round glass hanger full of fancy white benches and cafés. Next to the sausage and egg and beetroot at the buffet they were serving dried horse meat. I could tell, because on the sign it said 'Dried Horse'. Sean Walker, the *Guardian*'s long-time former Russian correspondent, was outraged when I pointed this out. Horse is apparently much more of a lunch dish.

At which point, sitting down with my tray of horse and eggs, heading back to Moscow still a bit blissed out on England, I fell asleep sitting upright on my stool. When I woke up I had no real idea where I was, or indeed where I was actually going. I looked at my boarding pass to work it out, but there were three of them in my pocket and I couldn't focus on dates and times. In the end I asked someone just to be sure. Samara, she said, and of course it was Samara, en route to Mineralnye Vody, where the air smelt different and dogs wandered around the airport. A formally dressed family shared their pistachios with me as we waited, and on my laptop I tried to compose and really nail my thoughts on Jordan Henderson's role in an overly isolated central midfield.

England's happy game was done. But the aftermath was still playing itself out. In London a group of people had trashed an IKEA store. A crowd had been filmed leaping up on top of an ambulance, denting its roof. A parked police car had been surrounded and attacked. The next day Justin Timberlake would shout 'It's coming home!' from the stage of his sold-out concert in Birmingham. A nice gesture, but I don't remember seeing him at Malta away, the massive plastic.

There were eight days of this World Cup to go and four games in total. As a very fat man in a soiled chef's outfit moved through the fug of Mineralnye Vody departures lounge handing out samples of a delicious, vividly red Russian sausage, it was hard to accept all this really was going to end.

12

Waiting for the Great
Leap Forward

7 July 2018

Moscow felt chilly and grey after Samara. Coming back from the airport the traffic on Smolenskaya Street stretched down towards the river in one of those sudden Moscow gridlocks. For once there was no hurry. Russia 2018 had a moment to clear its throat. Over the next three days the four remaining teams would regroup, tend to their bruises and prepare for the final push.

England were back at the forRestMix Club in Repino. France were already in Moscow, holed up at the Hilton as they had been all tournament. Belgium were further out of town at the Moscow Country Club. Croatia had returned to the dreamy lakeside Woodland Rhapsody Resort outside St Petersburg, the kind of place Victorian noblemen went to take the waters and die grandly of tuberculosis.

Waiting for the Great Leap Forward

It was a natural break for everyone concerned, a time when the host cities beyond Moscow and St Petersburg began to pack away the bunting, when the whole travelling machinery seemed to shift a little, to streamline for the final phase.

The World Cup had turned notably European in those last few days. Bundled together, the World Cup's four semi-finalists covered a combined 0.52 per cent of the planet's surface. Almost all of it was lodged together up in the north-western corner of Europe, including our own Brexit-bound island. The Schengen Zone was bossing the knockout rounds. The great global tournament had become an internecine affair.

Twenty-eight teams had come and gone in the last twenty-four days. I'd seen many of them in the flesh and watched the others from some bar or airport or sofa somewhere in Russia. It seemed odd how many had seemed to brush across the face of the tournament, while others became deeply involved.

The continental divide was obvious here too. Africa had played out its worst collective World Cup since 1982, with not a single African nation making it through to the knockout rounds. African teams lost ten of their fifteen games and won just three. There is of course a degree of folly in grouping nations together like this. Africa is not a country. Algeria and Tanzania, for example, share a tectonic plate. But there is no reason to assume they should share much else. And yet what African football nations do share is an export model, a passion for football and a stream of talent

187

that operates as a feeder system for European clubs. There are strong domestic leagues. But all African players will emerge within this prism and are to some degree a commodity for sale. It can't help.

Egypt were the great African hope, but Mo Salah's shoulder injury and a lack of recovery time after the Champions League Final made him a peripheral figure. Salah had scored seven and made two of Egypt's goals in qualifying. But he wasn't right in Russia and the African champions went out meekly. Morocco were unlucky, going down in the last minute to Iran in their first game, pushing Portugal back in their second but losing to a Ronaldo header, then failing only narrowly to beat Spain.

Nigeria were the youngest team at the tournament, with comfortably the coolest retro kit. They came within four minutes of escaping the Group of Death. There was a togetherness to this Nigeria, but a lack of flair too. Tunisia scored goals but were poor overall. Senegal were also unlucky, going out by dint of having suffered more yellow cards than Japan, an asinine ruling that FIFA really should change. It was a shame. Senegal had looked the most convincing of the African teams, with star quality, depth and – it must be said – a sensational chorus-line-style team-warm-up routine.

After which it feels only right to offer a few words before we move to the endgame on the other teams at Russia 2018, the ones who haven't had much of a mention here so far. They came. They moaned about VAR. They went home. Often this kind of World Cup remains a private grief, a buried sub-plot one detail that stands out in the fug. And so briefly, in alphabetical order:

Australia

Finished bottom of a strong group. Tim Cahill still going, despite having spent the season kicking people in the Championship for a few minutes every fortnight. Feisty but disappointing, potentially 'brave'. Crying fans with inflatable kangaroos.

Costa Rica

Another physical, organised and occasionally violent Costa Rican World Cup. Bryan Ruiz took a penalty that banged down off the bar and cannoned in off Yann Sommer's head to earn a point against the Swiss. It made a lovely clanking sound.

Denmark

Good results, boring performances. A lot of defending plus Christian Eriksen. Another example of the small, prosperous European nation making progress. This is the currency of international football these days. Four million well-organised Nordics are a better bet than a wildly impassioned South American giant. Forget the ticker-tape. Where's the dossiers and the manager who never smiles?

Iceland

Yes, yes. Vikings. We get it. Iceland's success is often presented as a function of passion, fire, togetherness. In reality it is a paean to the merits of smallness, and of being rich. The most organised, rational, well-managed sporting nation in the world. But tedious to watch at this World Cup and easily beaten by Nigeria. The 'hoo' celebration is done.

Iran

Passionate, energetic, neurotically cautious and always doomed to lose out in a group containing Portugal and Spain. The goals that ultimately knocked Iran out were scored by Diego Costa and Cristiano Ronaldo, so presumably suffering for some wrong in a former life.

Japan

Went 2–0 up against Belgium, then lost 3–2 in the last minute after throwing everyone forward for a corner. Beyond that, nice, neat and entertaining in more orthodox ways. Had the politest coach in world football, Akira Nishino, who answered every question in minute detail to the extent there was talk of bringing provisions, water and maybe a temporary bivouac to his press conferences.

Mexico

Destroyed Germany, ran like green-shirted demons and had arguably the World Cup's most urbane manager in Juan Carlos Osorio. After the Germany game Osorio said the win was because of his excellent tactics. Then explained exactly why. At one point in that match Mexico had two players standing next to one another on the left wing as a weird kind of overload gambit. More people should do this, if only for the lols.

Peru

Got gushing treatment from the media, partly because their fans were absolutely everywhere, played fun music and were happy to do vox pops. Won their first World Cup game for forty years, but were strangled out of Russia by Denmark. Thereby freeing up a lot more space on the Moscow metro and in city-centre restaurants.

Poland

Doomed from the moment Kamil Glik, their best defender, injured himself in training trying to do an overhead kick. Torn apart by Colombia. Not the most interesting Poland. Which really isn't a very interesting thing to be.

Portugal

European champions, but yeah, no one really expected much. How can so many amazing technical footballers play with such a throttling level of tedium? Actually, that would make a good tagline for the team bus. Ronaldo beamed down from Mars and scored a hat-trick against Spain. Pepe and José Fonte, the two central defenders, left Russia with a combined age of 69. Ricardo Quaresma scored the goal of the World Cup, the outrageous outside-of-the-foot dink against Iran, a move he's only pulled off about 2,300 times in club football. But whatever Iran. You can't get YouTube.

How Football (Nearly) Came Home

Saudi Arabia
Dreadful against Russia. Somehow beat Egypt. Crown Prince Mohammed bin Salman showed up and got the full Vlad treatment. A forgotten green substance.

Serbia
Endured a political furore as two Swiss players with Kosovar roots scored against them in Kaliningrad and made the sign of the two-headed eagle, a reference to the war of independence in the 1990s. Lost more prosaically to Brazil in the group-stage decider. Very tall.

South Korea
Out after two games, but then knocked Germany out in the third. We'll always have Kazan.

Switzerland
Surprisingly vibrant, skilful and non-boring. Another part of the small, successful Euro teams hard core. But still lost to Sweden in the round of sixteen in arguably the least interesting-looking World Cup knockout tie of all time.

*

So that was them, the other guys. All of them had gone by the time the semis rolled around and Moscow began to take on a different feel. In between writing follow-up and previews and trying to make the washing machine in the flat work, I'd noticed England fans had begun to arrive. The numbers in Moscow were quietly thickening every day.

Waiting for the Great Leap Forward

As England fever took over back home the echoes in Moscow were tangible. There were emails and messages on Twitter from travelling fans, acquaintances and random readers asking about safety and logistics and, quite often, the weather. The day before the semi-final a group of Millwall fans from my part of London turned up via a series of tortuous connections. By the next day there was already a video of them on social media playing guitar on Arbat Street and singing the Millwall edit of 'Hey Jude' with a large group of delighted-looking locals (swap the 'Hey Jude' at the end of the na-na-na-nas for 'Millwall' and you're there).

Moscow was a fun, peaceful place in those few days, home to surely the largest contingent of English people in the city's history. But it was also crammed with Croats, French, Chinese, Americans and wanderers from every nation packing out the pavement bars and the public squares. It felt significant. Many English people had stayed away for fear of what they might find. But by now it had become clear that Russia 2018 was a Putin joint, that Russia was, in effect on lock-down, a safe space for the duration.

Not that Russia seemed that much clearer as a result. We knew we were being sold a piece of stage management from the first few days. There is no doubt Putin had decided to present a scrubbed and orderly face to the world. There would be no hooliganism. There would be no suppression of demonstration, mainly because demonstration had been banned during the World Cup. The police and army were present, but with a fixed grin. The stories of Russian officials being taught to smile on special courses may or may not have had anything in them. But they seemed misplaced. The Russians we met were grumpy, brusque, funny, bored, personable in equal measure, just like people in every other place on earth.

There had also been concerns from the start about the legitimising effect of all this glorious sport on Putin's semi-dictatorship. And it's true, Russia isn't a democracy. It's not concerned with civil rights, with diversity and the push towards pluralism. Not yet, anyway. For a while in Moscow during the World Cup there was a place called Diversity House, a building where LGBTQ football fans and people generally could go and meet and feel safe and welcomed. The idea was there to open one in St Petersburg too, but somehow this didn't happen. Not everywhere is quite as liberal as the capital. Two months after we left people were being beaten up in the streets by police for protesting against drastic pension reforms unveiled under cover of the World Cup.

Russians themselves are not simply subjects; they are distinct from all this. It is hard to be present and marry the two. One of my favourite memories from the edge of the World Cup happened in that period waiting for the semi-finals. I was standing on a pedestrianised street in the centre of Moscow in the wee hours when a young man and woman appeared, set down a hat and a CD player, drew a circle of passers-by, then performed a brilliantly athletic, fun, conservatoire-trained version of a Russian folk dance, whirling each other around, laughing between the moves, then finally bowing and waving and running off to cheers and roubles folded into their hat. This kind of thing happened just off stage throughout the World Cup. Skating across the surface of the cities you kept getting this feeling of a culture behind the culture, of Russia as a place with its own deep well of warmth, a place that you'd quite like your place to be like.

As Monday ticked around into Tuesday, the show kicked into gear again. It felt a bit like Christmas Eve as we filed into the basement room at the Luzhniki for Gareth Southgate's pre-match press conference. For England, this would be a first appearance at the grey concrete heart of this World Cup, but it was also a kind of homecoming. England had been shuttling around the Russian landmass for the last month. This felt like the stadium gig at the end of that provincial tour, something hard-earned and precious.

There was a crackle in the air as we prepared for our audience with Gareth. Necks were craned. The room was crammed to the far walls. A FIFA wonk fussed with the stage, adjusting the mics and water bottles. And finally there he was, striding in crisply, carrying a kind of energy with him now, strangely luminous. Journalists from other countries jostled with the English press to put questions. Answers were patiently transcribed, clarified with sub-questions. The same Southgate who had at one point seemed like a patsy, a pressed-man, a plot device, was out there now high above the world, the papers wanting to know whose shirts he wears. Southgate was calm, of course. He talked about his pride in the players, about the things they'd learnt and the fact they expected to get better. At the end he was asked about 'It's Coming Home', which was still everywhere, which had by now become a standard greeting, a sign-off from emails, a part of the everyday vernacular. 'I couldn't listen to it for twenty years, frankly,' Southgate said, mildly. 'It has a slightly different feel for me. But it's nice to hear people enjoying it again.'

A few hours later it was time for the first semi-final. France and Belgium were playing in St Petersburg. I watched it in my favourite bar close to our flat. France had thickened their midfield out, playing Blaise Matuidi in a deeper role, where his energy nullified the power that had helped Belgium overwhelm Brazil. Belgium had Nacer Chadli, a winger, at right-back and Jan Vertonghen, a centre-half, at left-back.

The only goal came from a corner, headed in by Samuel Umtiti. Later Kylian Mbappé produced an amazing little piece of skill on the right to put Olivier Giroud in on goal. Belgium were enervated. They couldn't get the ball. France were simply too good and still playing within their limits, like a boxer saving himself for the late rounds.

France's manager Didier Deschamps had been noticeably sullen at the Euros two years ago. In Russia he'd begun to give a little more. 'It's sport. We have this privilege to give happiness to the French people and the public,' he said afterwards. Asked about his own World Cup Final experience, victory in 1998 with France's rainbow team, Deschamps was fairly sanguine. 'You have to live in your own times: I never, never, never mention my own history. Some of them were not born but saw pictures. It belongs to a lot of French people that lived through it but not the young generation. I'm here to write a new page in history, the most beautiful page.'

13

The Reckoning

11 July 2018

Dum-du-du-dum-du-dum-dum.

Every game at Russia 2018 had kicked off the same way. The same music. The same bass line. The same involuntary nod of the head. From World Cup opener to World Cup semi-final, from Volgograd to Moscow, from the Queen of England to the hounds of hell, the song remained the same.

With five minutes to go to kick-off, the Luzhniki Stadium shivered a little under the lights. The sky above the lip of the roof had already turned deep blue. The players of England and Croatia had already been out for their warm-ups. The pitch was clear now. At which point those oddly comforting rituals kicked in. Put out the flags. Cut the PA. Let the air settle as the players start to mass in the tunnel. Then it's time for, well, you know what it's time for.

Dum-du-du-dum-du-dum-dum.

The Reckoning

Will it ever stop? Will we ever be free of 'Seven Nation Army'? Italy's 2006 World Cup winners were the first to adopt the White Stripes' most famous song as their personal tournament anthem. By the time Euro 2008 came around, that stomping riff and the clattery drums had become a pre-match staple, played in the moments before kick-off at every game from Innsbruck to Vienna. I remember hearing it bounce around the Ernst-Happel-Stadion for the first time, excited to be reporting at my own first tournament, and thinking, well, yeah, I could get used to this.

Ten years on those fat, thumping notes are stuck in my head for ever, imprinted by the force of repetition. '7NA' has been at the Olympics, cricket tours, rugby, darts, not to mention every football match everywhere. You wonder about the effect of these uninvited companion pieces, of spending your life with a bass line. A while back one of my kids was scrolling through the radio stations in the car and started playing 'Seven Nation Army' really loud. I had to turn it off. And park by the side of the road for a while, shivering. But no, really. I'm. Fine.

So of course 'Seven Nation Army' was back for England versus Croatia, a song that isn't actually about sport, or winning, or jumping on people's heads, but is instead about – big yawn – *the pressures of fame*. And yes, it's not actually a bass line but a guitar string tuned down because the White Stripes don't like having a bass. Plus the title is meaningless. 'Seven nation army' is what Jack White used to think the Salvation Army was called when he was a kid.

But it works. It is part of the weather of these occasions, the noise that always happens just before the other things happen. There were the usual giant flags at the Luzhniki as the music faded away and the players came out to line up down below us. The semi-final was a late kick-off, 9 pm Moscow time. But the whole World Cup felt late by now, its doomsday clock ticking closer to midnight.

The Luzhniki was sold out, with the crowd crammed right up into the gods on all sides. It is a huge open space, the distance magnified by the running track to create a great gurgling cauldron of air and noise. The red and white Croatia end was over to our right. England's travelling regulars had pegged out the usual ring of flags away to our left. This time around there were 10,000 latecomers crushed in after a scramble in the last few days that had seen Moscow suddenly flush with England shirts strolling the pavements and packing out the cafés.

By now the Luzhniki felt like a home fixture to me, a short hop down Line 1 from Kropotkinskaya station or half an hour's walk over the river and through Gorky Park.

To kill some time in the morning I'd wandered around the FIFA museum near Smolenskaya station. Inside, the bored-looking security outnumbered the visitors. The tone was predictably gushing. At times FIFA does seem fundamentally confused about its own role, apparently convinced that it 'gave' football to the world, that the sport couldn't exist without the bunch of piratical opportunists turning it into an orbiting cash dispenser. A picture of Gianni Infantino hung at one end, FIFA's egg-headed president looking benevolent, generous, wise, stern, and like the interim leader of the galactic space federation who, for all his talk of a trade deal to end the civil war, is still secretly in the pay of an evil dark lord in a metal helmet.

The museum was brilliant nonetheless. There were Pelé's boots from 1958, tiny and strange, in heavy shrivelled brown leather. There was the Jules Rimet trophy, the same model that the Italian World Cup organiser Ottorino Barassi had hidden under his bed in Rome during the Second World War to keep it from the Nazis. There was a tribute to Mexico 86 Diego Maradona, hair a perfect rumpled shaggy rock-star bouffant, gripped with an irresistible sense of destiny.

And this is the beauty of the World Cup. Throw whatever you like at it. Dunk it in greed, degrade it with corruption and self-interest. Drape it with the inanity of the sponsor-driven show. At its heart there is a kind of beauty that evades all this, and a game that remains somehow irresistibly pure, that you just never get to the end of.

Strolling through all this World Cup iconography, it was tempting to wonder what might happen if England did beat Croatia. The pictures from home were wild, Bacchanalian and drenched in a joyful escapism. That night there was a huge World Cup concert planned for Hyde Park in central London. The Lightning Seeds would appear on the main stage and sing about football coming home. There would be big screens and huge drunken crowds and shouts and hugs and people playing out those scenes again in the way those scenes tend to play out.

How Football (Nearly) Came Home

The last time England got to a semi-final of a World Cup all this was all very new. It felt like a genuine surprise even to those caught up in it. Italia 90 was a change of gear, the moment football began to transform itself from an outsider pursuit, something still associated with violence and grime, played in decaying grounds in post-industrial cities, to its current status as cash-drenched leisure-economy juggernaut.

Before that semi-final in Turin Italian police had penned groups of England fans in with baton charges as they left the railway station and no one really seemed to mind much. In the stadium there were rows of Union flags and a banner with the words 'Pay No Poll Tax'. The England fans had sunburn and old-school tattoos and tiny shorts, a different kind of tourist to the day-tripping, budget-airline lads of Moscow.

Back then the world was still an analogue place. Football was an event we waited for, counting down the hours, something that arrived via the terrestrial TV crews, crackly radio and a gaggle of newspaper journalists. This time around the World Cup was a constant shared happening, an experience that never went off.

For the England players, Fabian Delph's trip home to be present at the birth of his daughter seemed a genuine eye-opener. Delph had flown back in a private jet with Vincent Kompany's family and was at home for the Colombia game. He said the penalties had probably brought on his wife's contractions.

'Going back was incredible,' Delph said. 'The support was absolutely amazing. Even people who are not into football, stopping me, shouting and telling me: "Make sure you bring it home." It was crazy, overwhelming.'

The players had spent Sunday with their families in Moscow. On the bus there had been a team playlist and a team singalong. One of the songs was, of course, 'Football's Coming Home'. And for a while it was hard not to feel a spasm of hope as that same old bass line kicked in at the Luzhniki, and everyone hunkered down for an occasion that really was just going to happen now, ready or not.

*

England's team was unchanged. There had been calls for Sterling to be dropped, if only because there are always calls for Sterling to be dropped, despite a fine performance against Sweden. Zlatko Dalić brought Brozović in ahead of Kramarić. Another defensive midfielder would give Luka Modrić and Ivan Rakitić a little more freedom.

Out on the Luzhniki pitch the players stood one last time, England in all white, Croatia in their deep blue and black squares. For the first time at this tournament, 'God Save the Queen' was sung with the familiar sea of spread arms, not so much a hymn of praise as a taunt, a fight intro. And so with a peep and a rolling wave of noise we were off, the air starting to fizz as Croatia played the ball around between them, heading back towards their own goal, interrupted by Jordan Henderson sliding in to bundle Rakitić to the floor.

England seemed to be running on adrenaline in those

early moments. Jesse Lingard went through the back of Strini. There was a minor squabble among the players, fingers pointed, chests poked. A few moments later England were running hard again, this time Lingard cutting inside beautifully and sliding a pass through to Dele Alli grooving through the middle. Modrić had no choice but to bundle him over on the edge of the area.

Kieran Trippier and Ashley Young spotted the ball twenty-five yards out, just to the left of centre. Looking at it a horrible thought occurred. This really was a good position. Danijel Subašić, Croatia's goalkeeper, looked weirdly positioned, too far to his right. What was he doing squatting over there, showing that huge bulging white-fringed target? Trippier took three steps, launching himself into a skip as he struck the ball, kicking up through it, straining for top spin.

Frankly it was never going anywhere else, hit flat and hard over the wall, then dipping just enough to zing down below the bar. The ball hit the top of the net and bulged it back. From the far end the bank of England fans had the perfect view and you couldn't help looking to them even as Trippier sprinted off to the touchline, caught by Kane and Henderson and submerged in a bundle of bodies.

It was a wonderfully pure strike. It was also the culmination of something for Trippier. By the end of the World Cup England's right-back would have delivered more crosses than any other player, a career high for another one of England's lost-and-founds, a player who was released as a kid by Manchester City for being too small, who found his way into the Premier League with Burnley, and who seemed to become ever more fearless as England went deeper into this World Cup.

In the press seats there were head shakes and disbelieving grins. It wasn't meant to happen like this. There was supposed to be pain and anguish and tension. Just after the re-start Sterling sprinted in behind the Croatian defence but was crowded out. England's attacking midfielders, their No. 8s, were finding space in front of the centre-halves. Alli drifted across the face of the defence with that air of aristocratic menace. Kane and Sterling almost wriggled through again. And for a few minutes in Moscow England were running on air.

It couldn't last. Croatia are a fearsomely tough footballing entity, from team to fans to undying shared spirit. The Croatia versus Turkey quarter-final at Euro 2008 is still the loudest single sporting event I've been to. At one point in extra-time I tried stuffing screwed-up bits of A4 in my ears just to block out the sound. On the way there my train carriage had rocked from side to side and bounced on its rails so violently it had to stop, a result of two hundred huge, beefy men in red and white shirts leaping up and down singing patriotic songs.

It has become a cliché to suggest the steel of the Croatia national team was forged in the fire of war, the ultra-nationalism of the Balkan conflict. But it is also true. Or at least, Croatia's players and fans seem to think it's true, which is pretty much the same thing. Watching them sprint angrily back into their defensive positions here, grappling with each other in the rush to cover and double-mark was an early sign of what would come.

A few things had fallen England's way. They were still the bad guys for a majority Russian crowd, but Croatia defender Domagoj Vida had done them a favour here. After the win against Russia Vida had been filmed shouting 'Glory to Ukraine', a soldier's call and response that became a rallying cry of Ukraine's resistance in the current armed struggle. It wasn't the only odd note. Dejan Lovren had been seen singing 'Bojna Čavoglave' in the dressing room after the victory against Argentina. 'Bojna Čavoglave' is an anti-Serb song from the Second World War that was favoured by the genuinely terrifying Ustashe, the kind of Nazis even Nazis admire for being particularly Nazi.

From the start Vida got huge boos and whistles whenever he touched the ball. The game became by turns open, sluggish and simmeringly violent. Lovren shoved Kane to the floor with both hands, but somehow got away with it. Vida was muscled aside by Harry Maguire at a corner and leapt up to snarl and shove his hands into the endless rolling landscape of the Maguire chest region.

With half an hour gone Kane somehow failed to score from ten inches out. Lingard played him in with a neat pass down the left, Kane scurried in on goal in that malevolent-hunchback style and side-footed the ball across Subašić, who blocked. From the rebound, a foot out and at a tight angle, Kane somehow punted the ball onto the post. Replays would later show that Subašić had got a fingertip to it. Kane bent double and gasped for a second.

Luka Modrić began to pop up a bit more often, keeping the ball, pushing passes around, and at one point dribbling in an elaborate zigzag past three England players like a cartoon mouse being chased by a broom.

Otherwise the game scrolled towards half-time, with a sense of energy being conserved. England were comfortable. But you got the feeling Croatia were working out their range and starting to read their limits. You see this in tennis with the better players. Lose a set, but lose it well, find the edges of your opponent's game and come sprinting out into the next one. Croatia walked off quickly at the break. The air was still, like a glass of fizz with the bubbles gone.

And so over to Gareth. In the days leading up to this game something had changed. Southgate had spoken for the first time about the possibility of actually winning this tournament. No doubt it was deliberate, a way of broaching the subject without allowing it to build its own tension. Southgate had talked about meeting the players of 1966, about the way that World Cup had hung over English football ever since. He suggested this one would be bigger because football is bigger, the game both a global commodity and a global obsession. All of which was true. But it still felt a parallel world away, even at 1–0 in Moscow with the hour getting late.

Everyone knew there were problems with England. The run to this stage had involved beating opponents well below the calibre of Croatia, and beating them while playing right up to the high-water mark of this England team's capacities. All week the feeling had been there that England had to find some other gears. The old problems with punting the ball forward and struggling to keep possession had been aggressively reined in. But at times you could still feel a clog in the heart of the team, a forced element in the new patient style, an awkwardness in the way the ball was transferred from midfield to attack.

Passes from the central areas had been slow in that first half, as they often were, always with a pause, a moment to look up. Jordan Henderson had worked like a Stakhanovite in Russia. But he lacked the ability to take the ball, turn, pass and find space with such speed you put an opponent back on their heels, those moments where it all becomes effortless.

This is nothing new. It is probably a cultural thing, an idea of how this game should be learnt and played, the skills prized from a young age. For example, in England it has become a kind of shared national bonding exercise to mock Mesut Özil, who seems to have spent most of his time at Arsenal being ferried around in his presidential litter by lesser players, a frail alien princeling beamed down into our midst to nudge and prompt and shrug his shoulders. But Özil is brilliant at exactly this skill, at making the pass that makes the other passes possible, at taking the ball without breaking stride in those transitions from defence.

Southgate had talked constantly about development. He knew better than anyone that while the details around this team, the mood, the attitude had been decisive, the players were still punching up. Of the four semi-finalists, England had the least technically refined group of footballers. There were no England players with the high-end skills of Hazard, Pogba, De Bruyne, Mbappé, Modrić or Rakitić. Success had brought a hiatus from the usual toxic attack by fans and media, followed by a ludicrously fawning degree of praise. For now at least, Southgate was untouchable. But as the balloon kept on rising there was a slight feeling of vertigo among those who had seen this process before.

Croatia came out like a train after the break. Rebić bundled Kyle Walker over. Mandžukić was booked for hurling the ball away as he argued about a free-kick. Vida smashed through Kane by the touchline, leaving him rolling in the advert boards. England looked wide eyed. Something was beginning to work on them, some other energy sticking to their limbs.

With sixty-eight minutes gone Croatia found the equaliser. Vrsaljko dumped a long, swirling cross into the England area from the right touchline. Walker bowed down to head it away but waited too long. Perišić arrived at speed behind him, raised a foot and pinged it into the net off the sole of his boot, shaving Walker's ear in the process. A huge roar emerged from that end as the net billowed. It had been coming.

And it was almost lights out three minutes later as England staggered and stumbled and John Stones scuffed a clearance out to Perišić, whose shot clanked against the far post. England were unable to find any rhythm. Modrić was key to this changing tide, sliding the ball into the most painful little avenues of space, every touch of the ball informed with some special kind of intelligence, a thirty-two-year-old who would end up running further than any other player at Russia 2018.

Everyone knows Modrić's story by now. There was the horror as a child of his grandfather being murdered by Serbs near his home, the family fleeing across the border and taking refuge from the war in the Iž Hotel in Zadar, where young Luka played football endlessly in the hotel car park. We know about the extraordinary promise, the poverty, the wooden shin-pads made by his father, something Modrić himself has said he doesn't remember. Too delicate to make the step up, he got his edge playing in the horrendously physical Bosnian league. Arsenal, Barcelona and Bayern Munich turned him down. But he kept on refusing to go away. Even after the first big move to Spurs Harry Redknapp was unconvinced and played him out wide. Real Madrid followed, and an occasionally painful start there, followed by a gathering supremacy as a peerlessly skilled all-round central midfielder. Modrić had four Champions League winner's medals by now. At that moment he was the best, most compelling footballer in the world, a small, un-starry, rodent-like figure, who seems in his basic movements to know just a little bit more about what's happening around him, the angles, the bounce of the ball.

Both teams dug in. Rashford came on for Sterling, who had once again run himself to a stop. England broke the length of the pitch and Lingard shot just wide. Pickford made an excellent save from Mandžukić. On ninety minutes Kane flashed a header wide from a free-kick, then bent double again as the whistle blew for full-time.

The Reckoning

Croatia were supposed to be tired. This would be their third consecutive period of extra-time. God knows everyone else was exhausted just watching. Up in our row no one said much. The end was very close now one way or another. And as extra-time kicked off England did throw their last reserves into this. Eric Dier came on, to no obvious effect. John Stones had a header cleared off the line. Right at the end of the first period Pickford made another wonderful save, hurling himself into a starfish shape to deflect Mandžukić's point-blank shot over the bar.

The players traipsed off at half-time of extra-time. As they swigged and spat and bowed their heads to listen to Gareth, it was hard not to think of his own remark about Sven-Göran Eriksson in similar circumstances. Southgate was there in Shizuoka the day England went out of the World Cup to the ten men of Brazil in 2002. 'We expected Winston Churchill,' he said of Eriksson's half-time team talk. 'Instead we got Iain Duncan Smith.'

Southgate was embarrassed when this came out. It was supposed to be a private remark. He has since disowned it. And it doesn't really sound like him, or at least not like the mature, waistcoat-era him.

Against Brazil all those years ago England had been eaten up by a better team, deprived of the ball in the heat, made to chase. For the last half-hour something similar had happened here, the passing of Croatia's midfield and their manipulation of the ball in tight spaces taking the game away. This required a different kind of intervention. Oratory was never likely to be enough.

How Football (Nearly) Came Home

For all his qualities Southgate was yet to show at this World Cup he could react in that way, plunge his fingers into the game in front of him and pull it into a different shape. He was limited by the players at his disposal. Southgate had watched England's last World Cup semifinal against West Germany in 1990 at a mate's house with a curry and some beers, albeit even then as a teenager taping all the games, watching them back, trying to learn from what the players did.

The difference is that England really should have won that game in 1990. At times they had the world-champs-in-waiting hanging on. That team was more mature. Look closely and it was crammed full of creative talent, rippling with possibilities. The England of Lineker and Beardsley, Barnes and Waddle, Gazza and Platt would have fancied its chances of winning the World Cup against a moderate Argentina in the final. Hence the tears, the feeling of chances missed, the stage play, the documentary film, the folksy myth. Hence, in part, the elegiac schmaltz of 'Football Coming Home'.

At the Luzhniki England were the better team in the first half. But by now they were being suffocated, teased into showing their own limitations. The midfield seemed constantly outnumbered. The full-backs were being pushed into their own half. On the ball, in the clinches Croatia looked superior. How to staunch this? Southgate might have put on an extra central pivot, might have switched formation to the newly fashionable orthodoxies of 4–4–2. But this system had got England here and Southgate is a systems man. England were level in the game. A change could give more space to Croatia, could unbalance a defence that was just holding on. Southgate stuck, didn't switch it. England's path was set.

It was heavy going for everyone. In the row of seats in front of me a middle-aged man smoked an illicit cigarette very quickly under his desk, grimacing at the agony of high-stakes international sport, and perhaps also at the lung-crippling draughts of tar required to get it down him before anyone noticed. I drank half a bottle of lukewarm Diet Coke very quickly for the caffeine boost. On balance, half a valium might have been more useful

England's players walked back out with a round of hand-slaps and chest-bumps. Off to our right the England end had gone more or less silent, hostage instead to the thudding and thumping of the England band. We had been spared this until now. To widespread relief the band had not been a fixture at this World Cup. That plodding bass drum had been a soundtrack to so many unhappy occasions in the recent past there were plenty of people willing to attribute the lifting of the mood, in part, to their absence. Here they were back, the drone picking up, filling the silence, bedding it in as the game kicked off again.

It took four minutes for the night to tip one way. England failed to clear a high ball. Perišić leapt above Trippier on the edge of the area and headed the ball back in. England's defence froze, just long enough, didn't track the runs, seemed for once paralysed by the moment. Mandžukić hadn't done much in the game before now. But he is a brilliantly seasoned player, veteran of Bayern Munich's all-conquering Champions League-winning team and a serial title winner with Juventus. Mandžukić is fearless, too. He took two steps towards the ball and didn't just slot or place or poke or pause, but smashed it low past Pickford into the bottom-right corner.

A photo of the goal would appear everywhere in the next few days showing Pickford diving, England's defenders static and Mandžukić veering away even as he plants the ball into the net. It looked like that in the moment, a tableau that seemed to stretch out, imprinting itself in the memory. And then the players were off, the blue and black shirts writhing and tumbling by the corner flag, knocking over a photographer, grabbing each other by the shoulders and the hair.

The Croatians on that side roared. Some ripped their shirts off and whirled them around their heads. Beneath it you could just about hear a kind of sigh. This was done. Everyone could feel it.

Southgate brought on Jamie Vardy for the last six minutes of the one hundred and twenty. Trippier limped off, leaving ten white shirts on the pitch. Pickford gathered a loose ball, tried to throw quickly and almost sparked a mass brawl as Croatian players blocked his way. And as the game slid into stoppage time of extra-time, England were awarded one final free-kick, a chance to load the box with that old white train. Not this time. The kick was floated in, a horrible, tired brick of a thing. Perišić ran upfield with the ball at his feet, and suddenly that was that.

The Reckoning

The blue shirts danced and hugged each other as England players crumpled down on one knee, hands on the turf. Rashford sobbed. Alli sat holding his head. In the middle of it, Gareth strode out and shook hands with Zlatko Dalić. There were little hugs and backslaps for his players. Ashley Young was hauled up off the floor.

In an odd kind of way this was Southgate's best moment in Russia. England had lost. But, well, it was fine. This was a defeat that felt like defeat, and not like something more, not a disaster, or a slight, or a farrago of blame and shame, or anything anyone has to feel bad or sad about.

The England fans stayed in their end, still singing and clapping. After a while 'Don't Look Back in Anger' began to boom out over the stadium PA, echoing around the empty stands. It turned into a singalong, cheerful in that distinctly English way where sentimental, minor-chord things somehow sound uplifting and defiant. Before long Southgate and the players were over on that side, waving and clapping for what felt like hours, a moment that nobody on the pitch or up in the seats or looking on from our side seemed to want to end.

14

This Is the End

16 July 2018

And so, fade to grey. No plans for final day. Stay in bed, drift away.

Or perhaps things would be a little different this time. As Sunday slid into Monday the fallout from England's defeat in Moscow felt lighter than expected, less terminally mawkish. There had been times during the endless World Cup summer of 2018 when it was impossible to escape 'Three Lions', or 'Football's Coming Home', or whatever the song is actually called, when the obsession had seemed to be at fever pitch.

But in the days that followed there was a kind of calm. The images from the Luzhniki were fond and fun rather than painful. This still felt like an occasion to be digested and marvelled at a little, if only for its rarity.

Did you see the England fans at the end bowing and

216

waving and cheering at Gareth Southgate? They didn't look broken by all this, or cursed with ancestral bad luck.

And did you see the people from London and Birmingham and Portsmouth in the pavement bars in Arbatskaya Square, central Moscow? They weren't distraught. They weren't spoiling for a fight. They seemed very thirsty. But they were happy too, or at least happy about the things they'd seen at the World Cup. We've got to go home now, people kept saying, with a shrug or a laugh. And football wasn't coming home with them. But that was fine.

Did anyone really weep about this, in the way they were supposed to, in the way the day had been set up? There was a photo that did the rounds at the time of two women in central London at the Hyde Park do with Saint George's Cross-painted faces, consoling each other in a way that looks almost too good to be true. It seemed too sad, too perfectly captured. Look a bit closer and maybe they're just tired. Perhaps they're wondering why they bothered with the face paint, or thinking about the night bus home, work tomorrow, life cranking into gear again.

Maybe the legacy of this World Cup might be to break the cycle. It might even involve not having a legacy at all. For England Russia 2018 was fun, thrilling, silly, escapist. And for once it felt as though the heaviness and the angst was left behind somewhere else. Let's face it there has always been something odd about England and football and decay and glory and all that coming home balls. This goes hand-in-hand with the strange presumption that England should win, that England not winning is a perverse derogation from some ideal state, and that constant 'root and branch' reviews are necessary to get to the bottom of this aberration. It makes little sense in a world where others also want to win, where others may simply be more efficient and better planned, luckier, more deserving.

In the middle of this the state of mournful hand-wringing has felt like a formal thing. The rituals are set. Flags, crying, bad luck, streaked face paint. Like so many things to do with English football and indeed Britain generally, it is a beautiful kind of sorrow, a cinematic angst, defeat as an industry. Just as 'Football's Coming Home' is really about loss, drift and a keenly cherished kind of sadness.

This is not a one-off. At bottom all the England football songs are about some kind of sad, doomed interaction with the outside world. My own favourite England tournament song is 'This Time (We'll Get It Right)' by the 1982 World Cup Squad. 'This Time' starts off jauntily. There is a defiance in the players' voices as they sing the verses and chorus together. But the lyrics make no sense. Even before the thing has started the 1982 World Squad are already angry and sad, brimming with anguish.

'This time!' they sing. 'This time! More than any other time!' Yes, this time, finally, finally, after all those other times, they're going to get it right, going to find a way, finally this time. Except it doesn't add up as England had actually won the World Cup just sixteen years before. They'd only played in one tournament since then, Mexico 70, and done OK. Where was all this unearned angst, this self-generated pathos coming from? Sixteen years of pain?

Wait till you get to fifty. Then let's have a talk. Standing there with your boot-cut slacks, your glowering moustaches, so innately drawn to loss and sadness.

Perhaps it was the same impulse, but with England out it was a relief not to have to think about trying to win a World Cup any more. The certainties of 1966 had hung over everything for as long as I can remember, branded across the popular culture. England 1966 is an immovable object, an exhibit to file past, like the mummified visage of Lenin. Nobby dancing, some people on the pitch, Roger Hunt nodding and raising his arms and running away as Geoff Hurst's header crashed back up off the goal line. It felt like an act of insurrection even to approach this, like walking up those steps and reaching out to shake the Queen's white gloves with a muddy paw.

Well, it wasn't going to happen now. Three days after Croatia England lost 2–0 to Belgium in St Petersburg in the third-place play-off. They were outplayed completely in the first half, and outplayed just a bit in the second. Belgium put out the first team. And at times you could see the joins with England. It felt like a Premier League game, but not an evenly matched one, a top-four team against a mid-table striver.

*

This just left the endgame. Moscow was sunny and breezy on the morning of the final. I went and had a final lunch with Jonathan Wilson, Nick Ames, David Hytner and Shaun Walker at Strelka, on the river by the park. It's a really lovely spot down there, with the spire of Christ the Saviour looming up on the north bank, the gold-domed cathedral that was turned into a swimming baths during the Soviet years when God ceased to exist for a while. The place was full of German TV types and well-to-do-looking Croats in shades and suit jackets. People talked about flights home and lay-overs and airport time.

In the event the final brought us one of the performances of the tournament. Although not on this occasion from Will Smith, who headlined the pre-match closing ceremony, performing the official World Cup song before the Luzhniki Stadium crowd. A shiny stage had been rigged up in the centre-circle for the occasion. Costumed performers capered around the fringes. A group of people in gold baseball hats and baggy trousers performed an inappropriate buttock-waggling dance. And finally there he was, the great Will, running on in a spotless white suit like a rap Willy Wonka. There was a cordial round of applause as he mugged into a camera before sprinting back off with indecent haste.

Smith wasn't the only star in the house. Two days before the final Gianni Infantino had turned up at his final World Cup press conference wearing a crisp new volunteer's hoodie over his lustrous presidential suit. Russia's volunteers are unpaid. Infantino is on £1.4 million a year plus perks to run FIFA. His plans at the time of the World Cup included staging an entirely new set of FIFA tournaments funded by a mystery $25 bilion investment fund. But the hoodie was a nice touch.

At the Luzhniki Infantino was in alpha company again.

Putin himself had come, bookending the tournament after his only other public appearance at the opening game. Emmanuel Macron was there and Croatia's president Kolinda Grabar-Kitarovi in a team shirt and white jeans, looking quite a lot more fun than every other grown-up on show.

Philip Lahm and someone called Natalia Vodianova, introduced as 'supermodel and philanthropist' (yeah, me too), walked out carrying a fussy-looking, multi-hinged suitcase. The case popped open to reveal the World Cup trophy itself, looking a little surprised and embarrassed and naked wearing just the green trim round its base.

Ivan Rakitić had predicted that Croatia would have 'four and a half million players on the pitch' in the final, which would almost certainly have been a breach of playing regulations. In the event the Croats had to settle for packing out the stands, by far the noisiest presence in the ground. On the pitch, however, it would be pretty much all France.

Although not at first, as Croatia began with some fire. N'Golo Kanté was booked for pulling down Ivan Perišić. Croatia had a grip of midfield. Modrić carried on where he'd left off against England, finding angles, keeping the ball, scurrying off down the flanks.

For forty-five minutes they were close. Somehow, though, France always seemed to have strength in reserve. They took the lead after eighteen minutes. Antoine Griezmann fizzed a flat free kick into the area and under pressure Mario Mandžukić flicked the ball into his own net trying to clear. It was a sickener for Mandžukić, hero of the semi. But Croatia had been behind in that game too, and they came back here as they had before, equalising ten minutes later through a brilliant finish from Perišić, who skipped away from Kanté and hammered a bouncing ball across goal into the corner.

The Croatia bench rose as one, running onto the pitch and punching the air. It was as close as they got. France scored again before half-time, Griezmann converting a penalty after an unfortunate handball decision against Perišić. From that point they just eased away as the rain started to fall, lightly at first and then in great drenching waves.

'In many respects, we are a miracle,' Zlatko Dalić had said in the build-up to this game, referring in part to Croatia's lack of investment, youth structures, modern coaching programmes or anything to explain logically the emergence of so much talent. This French generation were the exact opposite, their success in Russia tribute to the system behind them.

France exports more players than any other European nation. Technically refined, tactically aware players just seem to pour through Clairefontaine and its network of academies around the country. This team had been called 'the boys from the banlieues' because of the high ratio of players from the Paris suburbs. Often the descriptions seemed to paint them as a bunch of urban foundlings, wild things, escapees from the street. Whatever the reality of that, they are also products of a wonderfully well-tuned system, emerging at this tournament as a complete modern team, so good on the ball, so disciplined, so full of speed and purpose.

As wind whipped across the stadium France poured it on in the second half, stretching their shoulders a little. Paul Pogba and Kylian Mbappé made it 4–1. Mandžukić pulled one back thanks to a horrendous mistake by Hugo Lloris, who tried to play a clever little pass as he was closed down and simply kicked the ball onto Mandžukić's leg in front of goal.

As the game wound down Croatia looked spent, seven games into the tournament, three of which had gone to extra-time. At the final whistle there was a roar from the tricolour end as France's entire squad came sprinting out to join the team bundle. The striking thing was how young they were, ten of them in their early twenties, a genuinely brilliant store of talent still waiting to be unlocked. Down below us Didier Deschamps linked arms with his back-room staff in a tight circle and they huddled over, bouncing up and down together. Deschamps had been a grouch two years ago at the Euros, hard to like, spiky and snippy in his public appearances. In France he'd been criticised heavily for his defensive style with all that brilliance at his disposal. It was impossible not to feel happy for him now.

It was time to eat a final generic industrial caramel and nougat bar, to line up the vacuum-packed peanuts and try to write some appropriate words at the end of all those other words. Thankfully Russia 2018 kept giving right to the end, providing us with an unforgettable final tableau.

The day was still muggy but the skies around the Luzhniki

were filled with forks of lightning as the presentation stage was rigged up. Within seconds of stepping outside every dignitary present, including the president of France and the prime minister of Croatia, was utterly drenched, shirts stuck to their skin, rain running down their hair and into their eyes. All except one. From nowhere a large secret service-issue umbrella had appeared behind Putin as he walked out, presumably provided by the Kremlin's chief designated presidential umbrella operative. The World Cup ended with Putin standing alone being sheltered from the rain, still strikingly tiny and grave, the wings of his umbrella fanned out above the presidential head like Batman's cape.

The trophy was hoisted in a barrage of fireworks. France were deserving winners. The players didn't top any of the obvious metrics. Lucas Hernandez and N'Golo Kanté were near the top in tackles and interceptions. No surprise there: Kanté is like a one-man Bletchley Park, an early-warning device, seeing the angles, leaping in to fill the space. Mbappé was the outstanding young attacking player, but in Deschamps' system his brilliance was shackled to the right-hand flank, used as an impact runner, a means of penning a full-back in his own half out of pure fear. But they were by some distance the best collective, and a minor rebuke to the star system of club football. Best of all this France were a team that still seemed to be going somewhere, evolving into its final form.

Elsewhere Croatia had defied the predicted script. No one else really joined them. Well-organised European nations continued to produce the best teams. South

America continued to flounder in this shadow, along with everywhere else when it comes to the global game. A competition that used to alternate between Europe and the Argentina–Brazil axis had now been won four times in a row by Italy–Spain–Germany–France. All of Western Europe is in that line-up. With the exception of that awkward little island, of course.

England would head back to an affectionate welcome that seemed to come from a slightly different place to the delirium of 1990, Gazza's plastic breasts, crowds at the airport and all that. But then the world, and the World Cup, have both changed. This feels like a matter of scale and altered perspectives. It became a reflex to describe Russia 2018 as perhaps the best World Cup ever. It is impossible to say whether this is true or not. They say Sweden 1958 was pretty good, not to mention Chile 62, Mexico 70 and USA 94.

What is certain is that it was a brilliant World Cup, epic in scale and relentless in its drama, five weeks that seemed to stand outside of everything else around it. Russia 2018 also felt like the end of something, a final gasp before it into deep storage. The World Cup did regain some of its lustre. But this was also the moment we passed into something else.

The next European Championships in 2020 has already been transformed. It was Michel Platini's idea to make this a Euro of all the nations, staging matches all over the place from Baku to Copenhagen. UEFA will make more money doing it this way. Platini himself is currently banned from football for accepting a 'dishonest payment' from

Sepp Blatter. His legacy is this blank of a tournament, a cash-in a blur in the calendar.

Beyond that we have the next World Cup, Qatar 2022, companion piece to Russia. This will be the first ever winter tournament. Nobody knew this at the time, including the other people bidding. It will take place in a bespoke leisure-park network, a nation about the same size as Wales pouring irretrievable human wealth into its own vanity project.

Qatar had a powerful marketing presence in Moscow. The day before the final I walked down to Gorky Park to see the World Cup 2022 installation, which turned out to be a large frightening black cube floating on the Moskva River. The cube had been installed by The Supreme Committee for Delivery and Legacy, a Qatari body in charge of presenting an open, accessible face to the world; albeit one that might, on balance, have started off by giving itself a slightly more friendly sounding name.

The black cube had mirrored glass walls, discreet security at the doors and a queue of curious Muscovites stretching back along the river bank. It looked like the mountain hideaway of a comic-book super-villain, or the kind of structure that turns up on cable TV history programmes called things like 'Secret Nazi Super Palaces'.

In reality it was, according to its press release, 'the world's first floating multimedia museum', and a popular, if slightly odd-looking exhibit for the thousands of World Cup tourists. Looking into its mirrored sides on a grey Moscow afternoon it was hard to make out what this was supposed to mean. It looked like some opaque, mirrored future. It looked a bit like death.

Meanwhile the committee could be seen marching around the FIFA hotel. The Emir was present, hobnobbing with Putin. Qatar's Word Cup was sold by its bid team as a World Cup for the region, a unifying force in the Gulf. This hasn't really worked out. From June 2017 Qatar has been formally shunned by Saudi Arabia, Bahrain, the UAE and its immediate neighbours. Saudi's latest idea is to dig a canal all the way across Qatar's border, turning the peninsula into an island, its own mirrored cube adrift on the waters. Qatar needs the World Cup more than ever. This is only going to get stranger.

For now it was back to Moscow Sheremetyevo. The Monday morning after the final brought the most astonishing traffic meltdown I've ever seen as the massed hangers-on made a dash for the exit. And after that . . . well, there was no after that. Time to strip the hoardings. Russia 2018 was being disassembled, banners junked, volunteers decommissioned, flags packed way, oppressive regulatory laws reinstated.

Russia had been vast, impassive, warm, austere and fun and often opaque. After thirty-five days spent circulating around the same shared summer carnival we were gathered in the last departure lounge: the Mexican TV crews, Danish radio, Chinese newspapers, the administrators, volunteers, technicians, fans, ticket scalpers, tourists, hagglers, hustlers, men and women of the written press.

That moment had passed. It was gone, already packaged

up by a thousand highlights reels and souvenir supplements. It was time to board one last flight and scatter like an arrow shower to different corners on different planes, done here but never forgotten.

Acknowledgements

Thanks to Jack Fogg for having a great idea in the first place and for both patience and expertise in getting it done. Thanks to David Luxton for making it all happen.

Thanks to Will Woodward and Kath Viner for sending me to Russia and then being OK with me writing this. Special good vibes, warmth and thanks to Paul Johnson for all the advice, help and inspiration so far, and all the rest to come.

Thanks to Marcus Christenson and Jon Brodkin for being good cop, good cop. Thanks to top *Guardian* flatmates Stuart James and David Hytner – we'll always have 'the Pain'. Thanks to Shaun Walker and Andrew Roth for patiently explaining things. Thanks to Jonathan Wilson for arranging many dinners, almost all of them in other cities several hundred miles away.

Thanks to the people who I enjoyed talking to and reading the words of in Russia and out of Russia, a group of colleagues from every paper who make the games and the travelling such fun.

Bibliography

I read these three (proper) books about Russia before the World Cup. They are highly recommended for genuine insight into a place I just skimmed across very lightly. Bits of all of them have stayed in my head and will have informed in some part bits of this book.

Hobson, Charlotte. *Black Earth City: A Year in the Heart of Russia*. Faber & Faber, 2017.

Pomerantsev, Peter. *Nothing Is True and Everything Is Possible: The Surreal Heart of the New Russia*. Faber & Faber, 2017.

Walker, Shaun. *The Long Hangover: Putin's New Russia and the Ghosts of the Past*. OUP USA, 2018.

Index

How Football (Nearly) Came Home

Index

Index

Southgate, Gareth x–xi, xvii, 1, 15, 25, 26, 27, 72–3, 121; appointment as England manager xiii–xiv, 37–8; Belgium group stage game and 105, 110, 130, 153; Colombia game and 105, 128, 130, 133, 134, 138, 140, 142, 144, 145, 147–8, 152; Croatia semi-final and 195–6, 207, 208, 209, 211, 212–13, 214, 215, 217; dislocates shoulder 63; first press conference as England manager xiii–xiv, 37–8; 'Nord' nickname 38; Panama game and 66, 67, 69–70, 75, 110, 128; penalty shoot-outs and 39, 131, 147–8; reaction amongst fans to success of x–xi, 170–2; ruthlessness 27, 38–9; set pieces and 41, 178; squad choices 19–21, 24, 25, 39, 51; Sweden quarter-final and 179–80, 182, 183; 'Three Lions' and 39; Tunisia game and 28, 37, 40, 41, 42, 50, 51; waistcoat xi, 134, 144, 172; 'Whole Again' and 170

South Korea 95, 192

Spain 6, 23–4, 53, 82–3, 92, 107–8, 112, 113–26, 129, 188, 190, 191, 225

Spanish Football Federation 23

Spartak Stadium, Moscow 22–3, 24, 25, 47–8, 95, 104, 126, 127–8, 132–48, 167

Stalingrad, Russia 30–1, 85 *see also* Volgograd

Starace, Achille 84

Sterling, Raheem xii, 21, 33, 34–5, 36, 37, 63, 69, 70–1, 72, 135, 136–7, 139, 141, 177, 179, 182, 203, 205, 210

Stones, John 33, 35, 68, 72, 97, 141, 209, 211

St Petersburg, Russia 15, 52, 55–6, 57, 58, 59, 64, 65, 155–9, 186, 187, 194, 196, 219

Strigino International Airport, Nizhny Novgorod, Russia 64–5

Subašić, Danijel 204, 206

Sweden ix, 65–6, 95, 153, 168, 175–85, 192

Switzerland 19, 24–5, 155, 192

Taylor, Danny 34

Teixeira, Ricardo 86

'This Time (We'll Get It Right)' (1982 England World Cup squad song) 218

'Three Lions' (song) ix, x, xiv, xv–xvii, 39, 129, 130, 170, 181, 196, 201, 203, 216, 218

Tielemans, Youri 100–1

Tite 56, 151, 157, 159, 160

TNT 87

Trippier, Kieran x, 33, 72, 137, 142, 143, 144, 177, 179, 181, 204–5, 213, 214

Tunisia 14, 15, 26–7, 28–42, 50–1, 61, 62, 67, 133, 169, 172, 188

UEFA 79, 120, 154, 225–6

Updike, John 106–7

Uribe, Mateus 142–3, 170